So You Want To Be A Wall Street Programmer?

Andrey Butov

ISBN: 978-1-84728-421-1

Copyright © 2006, Andrey Butov. All Rights Reserved.

ISBN: 978-1-84728-421-1

To my wife Victoria - my favorite person

Thank you darling

Contents

Who is this book for? 9

Disclaimer 11

Introduction 15
   What can I expect to be doing as a Wall Street programmer? 17
   Database Administration 19
   Quantitative Analysis 19
   Network Programmer 20
   Quality Assurance 21
   Release & Deployment 22
   Compliance 24
   User Interface Work 24
   Web Development 25
   System-Wide Architecture 26
   Maintenance Scripting 27
   System Administration 28
   Automated Trading Engines 28
   Support 29

Required skills and knowledge *31*
    Programming Languages *31*
    Client/Server Concepts *34*
    Multithreading *34*
    Databases *35*
    UNIX *36*
    Debugging Skills *36*
    Interpersonal Skills *37*
    What about financial experience? What do I need to know about stocks, bonds, and that Dow Jones guy? *38*

Finding a job *41*
    Résumé layout *41*
    So how do you find a programming job on Wall Street? *45*

The Wall Street job interview *57*

Fear of the code *67*

Salary and bonuses *71*

From 9 to 5? *79*

Office characters *83*
    The burned-out developer *84*
    The manager wannabe *85*
    The 'work-is-just-work' guy *87*
    The old-school über-coder *88*
    The faker *89*
    The developer who isn't *90*

Wall Street traders *93*

Large banks vs. small hedge funds *101*

The programming environment 121

Typical day - then and now 131

Random advice 143
    Your tools will suck ... get over it *143*
    For recent college grads - no one here is your mommy *144*
    Most projects will suck *145*
    Go out for drinks *146*
    Buy a good pair of headphones *147*

Interview with a Wall Street programmer 149

So, what now? 155

Who is this book for?

This book is for...

a) Folks who find themselves pulling together random bits and pieces of information gathered from various sources across the Internet in an attempt to form a complete picture of the daily tasks involved in the professional life of a software developer on Wall Street.

b) An experienced developer from another domain of the IT industry entertaining the idea of switching focus to the New York City financial sector.

c) A recent college graduate who defines a Wall Street career as the pinnacle of professional success.

...and finally, since you are reading this, this book is probably for

d) You.

Disclaimer

If, as you read this book, you sometimes sense a slightly cynical undertone, it is only partly intentional. I am not, by any stretch of imagination, the definitive expert on all things related to Wall Street programming. The information here comes from my personal experience in the trenches.

I began my career some number of years ago on Wall Street as a developer fresh out of college, and as I write this book, some years later, I am still writing code for Wall Street firms. In between, I've worked for various types of companies dealing with various types of financial instruments. I like to think that along the way I picked up a thing or two about working with headhunters, finding work as a developer for a Wall Street company, navigating through an interview (from both sides of the table), building and sharpening required programming skills, dealing with traders (urgh), and other things one can't really grok fully by scanning through bits and pieces of information found on the Internet.

If you consider yourself to be smart, you'll disregard everything you read here completely, and form your own opinions after you join me in the trenches of Wall Street software development.

If, however, you consider yourself to be pragmatic, you'll understand that there is a degree of truth in almost everything, and proceed to read what is written here, taking in every morsel of information with a proverbial grain of salt. You'll be much better for it when you step out of the subway station on the corner of Wall and William that first Monday morning.

Please note that 'Wall Street' is not limited to the geographical area covering the southern tip of Manhattan in New York City. Although technically, this *is* where Wall Street is located, programmers targeting the Wall Street domain, and working in the financial sector in general, are not bound to this geographical location. Many 'Wall Street' programmers work in firms that are nowhere near Wall Street. While Wall Street itself is home to many big name companies, satellite offices for some of these companies as well as the offices for various smaller financial firms are located throughout the island of Manhattan, as well as in other states like Illinois and Texas. Most financial firms, regardless of where they are geographically located, do much of their business on exchanges and in markets located throughout the world, so it is quite common to have developers who work for one company to be located in London, Japan or Sydney. In fact you may be called upon to spend time in some of these other offices in order to become better acquainted with the development teams working there and also to get a better understanding of the business as a whole.

The usual bit applies about my tendency to use the pronoun 'he' instead of 'she', and my absolute reluctance to waste the time and space to constantly write out 'him or her' simply to adhere to some arbitrary notion of political correctness.

Introduction

Hacking code, in and of itself, is an utterly useless activity. At some point, about 10 minutes after you write the first obligatory 'Hello World' program, the existence of code and the necessity of writing it starts being driven by the needs of some specific domain.

Whether that domain happens to be telecom, pharmaceuticals, embedded systems, game development, the porn industry, or the financial sector, as you mature and gain experience as a programmer in that domain, you begin to master two things. One is the ability to navigate the vocabulary and concepts of the given domain in order to map it into programming solutions, and the second, is the ability to manipulate the path of your career more or less in the direction you want it to go. In other words, you learn how to 'play the game'.

Wall Street is no different. A recent college graduate or an experienced developer coming into the area from another IT sector arrives with (hopefully) an iron-clad foundation of computer science knowledge, ready to battle his or her way through millions of lines of existing spaghetti code (actually, naive college graduates come ready to design and implement large, elegant systems from scratch...but they learn quickly). After some time, a Wall Street programmer learns almost as much about bonds, options, hedging, butterfly spreads, repurchasing agreements, and credit default swaps as the nearest mid-level trader. More importantly, the Wall Street programmer learns about headhunters, traders, quants, Wall Street specific interviews, salary negotiations, and Wall Street office politics.

While I can't force any financial knowledge into your head (not that you'd want me to anyway), I can provide some insight into the other topics you might be interested in as you decide whether or not you want to make a Wall Street cubicle your home for the next 10 years.

Let's go...

What can I expect to be doing as a Wall Street programmer?

Wall Street, like any other IT domain has its subsections. Some are more well-defined than others, but there are definitely niches that you can specialize in as you progress in your career. For the first set of interviews, the most specific thing you'll be seeking is a 'Programming Job on Wall Street'. When I graduated from college with a degree in computer science, the options in my mind weren't even as specific as that; I just wanted to find someone who would hire a C or C++ developer. Living in New York, Wall Street was the most obvious choice. At present, I would argue that Wall Street is, by far, the largest employer of software developers in New York. I have zero statistics to back this up, but I doubt that many would take the opposing bet.

My first position on Wall Street required me to write code that served as the communication layer between the internal systems of the firm, and various external exchanges and data feed providers, for purposes of sending trades, receiving prices, sending quotes, receiving confirmations, and so on.

As it turned out, this is a need that almost every financial firm has. Different firms call these modules of code by different names -

exchange interfaces, feed handlers, translators - but no firm is an island, and they all require processing of incoming, third-party data, and, in return, to send out their own data to the outside world. By sheer circumstance of this being the task of my first job, my subsequent employers on Wall Street, with few variations, all took me on for purposes of writing similar interface layers.

But don't get me wrong, there was variation. At various points in my career I did nothing but database administration, or user interface development, or back-office trade reconciliation (all Perl, all SQL, all the time). I even had the occasion to write an entire trade-capture system from scratch (alone). But in the end, the easiest position for me to get on Wall Street would require implementation of some kind of a communication layer between the company and the outside world. This is the niche that I have built for myself. My résumé is filled with terms like ISE, CBOT, EUREX, TradeWeb, BrokerTec, Reuters, and eSpeed. These things would be meaningless to an employer looking for a UNIX system administrator, but for the dozens of Wall Street companies looking for my type of skill set each day, their employee requirements mirror my qualifications to a tee, and they immediately register my experience as being something they are looking for.

That's not to say that this is the predominant type of work on Wall Street. As a programmer, you have choices. Aside from the 'feed handlers' I mentioned above, here are some other types of jobs filled by programmers in Wall Street firms.

Database Administration

Database administration is a very large niche in the Wall Street programming universe. Wall Street *is* information, and today, that information resides almost entirely in databases. Every company I've worked in, no matter how small, had at least one database administrator. Proper design, implementation, and maintenance of the DBMS, associated schemas, and the data itself is crucial to a firm, and a full-time, dedicated developer is usually hired for the task. Aside from the initial design and implementation of the databases, DBAs are responsible for various maintenance tasks, such as backups and synchronization (in both the production, QA, and development areas), managing the database access rules (with both human user logins, group logins, and application specific logins), and optimizing the ever growing set of stored procedures and views required by the firm.

Quantitative Analysis

A quantitative analyst (quant, for short), is responsible for deriving and implementing the pricing formulas and methodologies for various financial instruments. Although mathematical formulas for pricing certain types of instruments already exist (like the Black-Scholes model for pricing options), most firms have specific requirements that call for custom-built pricing formulas. As you can probably tell, this requires a developer with a thorough understanding of complicated mathematics, as well as a good understanding of the financial markets, the various financial instruments and their relationships. In some firms, quants are responsible for not only deriving the pricing formulas, but also for implementing them. This is sometimes done directly in parallel with the pricing engine built into the company's trading system, and sometimes simply through Excel and VBA. Experienced quants tend to pull in the highest salaries of all the technical folks on Wall Street, as it is not very easy to find a person who can not only write code, but also has a thorough understanding of the mathematics involved to effectively price an instrument.

Network Programmer

Every process on Wall Street runs as part of a larger distributed system. Monolithic applications are not the norm. Messaging layers must be built on top of an existing, well known networking protocol in order to make it easier for the various modules to communicate with one another. When first starting to develop a trading system from scratch, it will probably take you about three minutes to realize that having each module wait on a socket for a byte stream of raw data is not the way to go. The messaging layer should be abstracted away to a degree where developers can simply take a **Price** or a **Trade** object and send it to another module over the network (or to several modules at the same time, such as the case often is).

The messaging layers are almost always built on top of UDP with some sort of a redundancy and delivery insurance layer built on top. Most firms purchase off-the-shelf redundancy layers, but even those firms still find it useful to build an additional abstraction layer on top of this in order to facilitate application specific communication demands. You haven't felt pain until you sat through a four day debugging session, going through hundreds of thousand of lines of Rendezvous logs in order to track down a runaway network packet.

Quality Assurance

It may come as a surprise to some, but many Wall Street companies do not have a dedicated QA department. I consider myself lucky if there is at least one person on the payroll who is responsible for testing the code properly. More often than not, the problem is not one of having enough money in the budget to hire a dedicated QA crew, but one of actually finding the right people for the job. Developers are notorious for not wanting to test their code to the degree they should. It's just not that much fun compared to actually writing it. So it becomes very difficult to find people who are both technical enough to be able to understand the requirements of testing the system, and, at the same time, prefer to spend their days testing other peoples' code as opposed to writing their own. Still, dedicated QA specialists who form their careers in this niche, and are fairly good at what they do, usually pull in a heavy salary.

Release & Deployment

Even when your customers work for the same company as you, deployment is a hassle. In a ten-person firm, you might be able to get away with copying files to production servers and the individual workstations, but after two releases you'll begin pulling your hair out, before admitting to yourself that you need a better way of doing things.

But, what's the big deal? Can't I just copy that .dll and .exe from my bin directory, update a configuration file and be done with it?

In a large investment bank, with 10,000 traders, manual release is out of the question. Let me paint a picture for you. You have a system composed of twenty distributed components. Not all of these components are rolling out, but seven are. The seven modules going out and the thirteen already in production need libraries. Some of these libraries are shared by all the modules, but some are shared by only some of the modules. Not only do you have to worry about having the seven new modules be compatible with the thirteen existing modules, now you have to worry about having all of them be compatible with libraries which may or may not have all been included by the programmer submitting the release request.

And since you can't release a binary without building it, now you have to worry about the source code. Which CVS tag are you taking out? Is it on a branch? Is the code even tagged? What will you do if one module out of the seven fails to compile against a library that's in production? Can you release the rest of the modules without including that one?

Aside from the issues with the binaries, you also have to worry about the hundreds of floating application configuration files, database configuration files, system files, **cron** entries, and so on.

Add to that the factor of having to push this release out to thousands of workstations, and hundreds of servers in the window of a few hours allotted, as the local traders are leaving for home on your side of the world, and the traders in Japan are coming in for their day of work.

Oh yeah, and you still have to bounce the systems and make sure everything comes back up without incident. Sounds like fun doesn't it?

Compliance

Compliance departments are not programmer-heavy, but a fair amount of development work still needs to be done here; mostly database work. The compliance department is responsible for making sure the firm adheres to all legal standards set forth by various entities, such as the SEC (Securities and Exchange Commission). Their software deals with things such as recordkeeping, privacy, and document tracking issues.

User Interface Work

User interfaces need to be written for various internal applications, including trade capture systems, risk management programs, database and system monitoring facilities, and administration tools. Screens are written mostly for Windows machines, although many legacy UNIX systems still exist with screens that require regular maintenance and augmentation.

The languages of choice are Java, C#, and if you are unlucky enough to be stuck with a legacy Solaris based system, something like the old (and awful) X GUI framework. Trade capture systems typically need things like entry forms for various financial instruments, and data validation. Of course, if you are playing around with a properly distributed trading system, data validation should not be done anywhere in the GUI layer...but you'll never see a properly distributed trading system. In a UFO somewhere, Elvis and Bigfoot are coding one up right now.

Risk management systems are grid-heavy beasts, especially in firms that trade options. Their screens typically implement a lot of custom-drawn controls because of the different requirements of each firm, but in the end, you still need a screen capable of displaying a lot of information, in a grid form, possibly with charts and graphs, originating from a constantly updating data flow.

Web Development

This will not be the type of web development where you argue days on end with your colleagues about the benefits of using CSS over HTML tables. Web interfaces here exist purely for the purposes of providing information for internal use, in a quick and efficient manner, without having to build a dedicated standalone application. For example, a web interface might be used for displaying the current state of various distributed processes.

Most of the pages are plain HTML with simple CGI scripts responsible for fetching information from some database. A small number of firms do provide some kind of a service to their external clients through their websites, and this might entail some degree of design work, but these firms are far and few between.

System-Wide Architecture

Chances are that your first job on Wall Street will not be in a role of a system architect. Nevertheless, many developers strive to reach this point in their Wall Street careers. Naturally, experience with various trading systems, and a thorough understanding of the needs of the particular company is required to be good at this task. Depending on the firm, system architects can still do a fair amount of coding, although for most, the interest lies in the high-level design aspects of the job. If you take a job at a very small financial company, you may find yourself designing a system from scratch without ever signing up to do so. The work is complicated, as trading systems are ever-evolving with the needs of the firm, and the foundation of such a system must be flexible enough to accommodate all foreseen and hopefully, any unforeseen requirements.

Maintenance Scripting

Although I've yet to come across a firm where the need for scripting is so big that it would require hiring a dedicated person for the task, every firm has a fair amount of scripting tasks that need to be done. Shell scripts, Perl, and to a much lesser degree, Python, are used to accomplish everything from internal automation of administrative tasks, to reconciliation of trades and prices.

Certain firms develop their own, in-house scripting languages that are quire often similar to existing scripting language, but include facilities to easily achieve things important to the specific firm – such as sending data through the firm's proprietary messaging layer. Since development time in a scripting language is usually much faster (in the right hands) as compared to a compiled language like C++, scripts are used whenever a situation calls for a quick solution to a problem, or when you find yourself performing the same mundane, repetitive task manually.

Sometimes, when you spend hours on end in a code / compile / build / test loop, switching to a small project that only requires a quick script almost seems like relief.

System Administration

Come on! You know what systems administrators do. That's right. Well, they do the same thing on Wall Street.

System Administrators configure servers and workstations (both UNIX and Windows), create and maintain user accounts, firewall settings, and network configurations, and they tend to mumble a lot as they work (don't ask me why). Their tasks also require a fair bit of scripting (mostly shell and Perl). And like system administrators everywhere, they get yelled at about how much money the company is losing per minute after one of the servers goes down.

Automated Trading Engines

Phew! Times are tough. People are lazy. But computers don't need Starbucks breaks. I have an idea - let's get the computer to do all the trading for us! Well, easier said than done. No artificial intelligence here folks; too unpredictable. These are systems driven by very complex rule sets that are very well defined, and usually require regular tweaking.

There are also compliance standards governing things like having a machine do trading without human observation.

Still, there are things a machine can do better than a human...like identifying temporary errors in pricing spreads in an electronic market and taking advantage of the situation as fast as only a computer can.

From personal experience, these systems take a very long time to implement, they often don't work as expected when they are pushed out, and they require constant maintenance. In short, they are more trouble then they are worth. Still, these things don't stop companies from constantly trying to implement such systems. If speed optimization is your cup of tea, this might be something you'd be interested in.

Support

The vast majority of software written on Wall Street is for in-house use. More often than not, your customer will be your nearest trader (or a few thousand nearest traders), an employee in the back office, or your colleague in the next cubicle. In many cases, the primary developers of the software are expected to support their system to some extent. Larger firms, however, tend to have at least one additional layer of support acting as the first line of defense. This layer is responsible for handling 'easy' and 'typical' questions. Their responsibilities may include bouncing an unstable system, updating a row in the production database, managing trader backlash after a server crash (nerves of steel!), and reporting system issues to the responsible programmer (oxymoron?) for further analysis.

Required skills and knowledge

Do I have what it takes to cut it as a programmer on Wall Street?

Sure you do!

...but just in case...let's check.

Programming Languages

C++ is still the predominant language on Wall Street. Don't let anyone tell you otherwise. Whatever the current fad might be, most work on Wall Street requires a language that compiles down to an executable binary without the aid of a managing virtual machine. While Java, and to a lesser extent, C#, are both slowly gaining in popularity for some types of projects, trading systems put speed at the top of the list - sometimes almost to the point of sacrificing stability, and most certainly to the point of sacrificing development time and cost. It might cost a company an extra two men and four months of development time to get a system that is able to execute a trade a few milliseconds faster than the competitor, but it's worth it. This is why, for speed sensitive systems, if a language is used where the garbage collector decides to clean up a bit while your quote or trade is moving through the pipe, and this causes the data to arrive a bit later than it would have otherwise, it simply isn't acceptable. Developers outside Wall Street who work with hard real-time systems can probably relate. So C++ is the standard for the time being, and will probably be the standard for the foreseeable future.

Even with C++ itself, esoteric language features are almost always skipped. Template meta-programming nonsense has no place here (and if you figure out where meta-programming is useful in a practical environment even outside Wall Street, please let me know). Programming language parlor tricks like these are for computer journals and academic circles, not enterprise trading systems where each second of execution time decides not only your next bonus, but also how well the traders are going to look at you for the duration of your stay at the company.

That's not to say that you should limit yourself to only the most basic features of C++. You should be comfortable with templates in general, common design patterns (and not just Singleton), common issues arising from static instantiation dependencies, proper object instantiation in an inheritance chain (virtual inheritance and otherwise), problems arising from object copy semantics (especially with pointer members and copy-on-write implementations), smart pointers, exceptions, and virtual table concepts.

C is also heavily used. This is in part because of the need to maintain legacy code, and also because most third-party APIs are in C, and when you're writing trading systems that either need to get data from some outside source, or send data to some outside destination (as most of them do), you'll need to talk to these APIs. Suffice it to say, the ***extern "C" {...}*** qualifier is a common occurrence on Wall Street, and a developer dealing with code like this needs to be familiar with things such as cross-language linking semantics, memory alignment issues (such as padding of complex structures on the stack), as well as ***void*** and function pointers (a well accepted mechanism for calling C++ methods from within C callbacks).

Client/Server Concepts

As I mentioned before, Wall Street runs on distributed systems, and nothing is designed as a monolithic application. Knowledge of networking concepts is required, and so is an understanding of client/server application design. Since all the proprietary messaging systems here are built on UDP (TCP is not used because it is marginally slower, and because the requirement of multicasting is always present), at some point every developer has to deal with socket code (unless the socket abstractions in place are impossibly brilliant and require no maintenance). As such, one should be familiar with C level socket concepts such as ***socket()***, ***bind()***, ***poll()***, and ***select()***. In all likelihood, you will never use these directly unless your task is to actually build an abstracted messaging layer, but they are part of a computer scientist's basic foundational knowledge, and you will almost certainly be asked about them on the interview. How *do* you wait on a socket without blocking or looping?

Multithreading

This goes hand in hand with the client-server concepts. Part of implementing a client-server architecture is implementing the servers, and servers are, typically, heavily multithreaded processes. I say *typically*, because regardless of what you might have learned in academia, there is some brilliant code out there implementing high-throughput servers without spawning threads left and right. It's amazing what the mind can achieve with a little imagination and a complete disregard for the proper way of doing things.

Anyway, you should be comfortable with the basics of spawning a thread to deal with each client connection coming into the server so that the main thread is free to continue listening to subsequent client connection attempts. You should also be comfortable with synchronization mechanisms and other accessories surrounding multithreading. In short, know your ***pthread()***, ***fork()***, mutexes (and semaphores in general), as well as higher level concepts like Java method synchronization.

Databases

Know your databases as well as your SQL. Aside from knowing how to do a simple ***SELECT*** statement, you should know when stored procedures are useful, and when they can be a burden, what database indexes are (clustered and otherwise), and how table-level, page-level, and row-level locking differ from one another.

UNIX

On Wall Street, UNIX is still king. Aside from the newer and smaller operations, servers on Wall Street are running Solaris, and to a lesser extent, Linux. As a developer, you will probably have a Windows box on your desk, but you will definitely have access to either a local UNIX machine, or to a cluster of community UNIX boxes sitting somewhere in a server room. The traders will almost certainly use Windows to run their clients, but this is just one module in a highly distributed system, and everything else – from the module that gathers prices from a third-party feed, to the piece of code writing SQL to the database – runs on a UNIX box.

As a developer, everything from checking log files, to debugging core dumps, is done in a UNIX environment, and, as such, you should be comfortable with commands such as *tail*, *sed*, *grep*, *awk*, *tr*, and *top*. You will also not get far without knowing either **vi**, **vim**, or **Emacs** (and no, I won't tell you which one I prefer).

Debugging Skills

No, not the built-in Visual Studio debugger (although it will certainly not hurt if you know how to use this either). Debugging means taking that pile of bits called a core file, and forcing it into **gdb** or **dbx** (from the command line - things you care about never core on a machine with a windowing environment). You will not be spending all your time doing this (and if you get stuck in a company where you *do* spend all your time doing this...run), but when the situation calls for a debugger, it pretty much cannot be addressed with anything else but - so know your stuff.

Interpersonal Skills

I thought twice about writing this section. After all, being a programmer, I am almost by definition not the most sociable of creatures.

The lack of extraordinary interpersonal skills is not a big deal, but you are definitely in the wrong place if you expect to sit in a cubicle (you though you were going to get an office? hah!), coding away, and expecting everyone to leave you alone. Aside from other developers who will drop by to ask you questions from time to time, there are traders to deal with - and these guys do *not* speak techie. Time will come when you will learn how to 'dumb it down' a bit in order to explain how the latest feature in the trading system works, but to newly arriving developers who are not used to dealing with customers directly, it may come as a bit of a shock to see how little what you say actually resonates.

What about financial experience? What do I need to know about stocks, bonds, and that Dow Jones guy?

I know this is one of the primary questions on your mind. Admit it.

If you are coming in from another IT sector, or are a recent college graduate, no one will expect anything from you as far as knowledge of financial markets or instruments is concerned.

As you progress in your career as a Wall Street programmer, you will gain some level of knowledge through osmosis. Like any other area of computer programming, domain specific knowledge is a necessity, and it will come in time. As you continue to work in the financial sector, related terms and concepts will seep into your mind without you noticing. Having to work with computer-challenged traders and the various levels of business management will ensure this.

Certain companies, namely large, international, investment banks provide seminars and training sessions, ranging from beginner to advanced levels, and covering all possible topics. There are even training sessions specifically targeting IT folks who want to learn more about the business and the financial side of things. I find these seminars incredibly, mind-numbingly dull, and tend to learn more by addressing gaps in knowledge as I go about my daily programming projects. You may be different, and find these seminars to be the pinnacle of intellectual stimulation.

Well then...good luck with that.

Once you have a few years of experience under your belt, the story changes somewhat. Interviews will now contain at least a few questions covering the financial sectors you outlined in your résumé. At the very least, there will be references to key terms and concepts, and you will be expected to be comfortable with the topic of conversation. Still, even at this point, as a programmer, you will not be responsible for knowing the intricacies behind the pricing and hedging of esoteric financial products (unless you are shifting gears and are applying for a job where such knowledge is required). If you happen to have absorbed more than an average amount of financial knowledge along the way, good for you! It can only make your job that much easier.

In short, don't worry about your limited knowledge of the financial domain, and focus instead on improving your programming and analytical skills. This is where your strengths lie, and this is what will be your primary leverage in getting that Wall Street job.

Finding a job

Résumé layout

This isn't entirely Wall Street related, but since I get so many requests for résumé reviews from folks looking to get a job on Wall Street, I though I'd add it here for kicks. I know as much about effective résumé layout design as I do about fixing cars - that is to say, nothing at all. What I do know is that my own résumé has yet to fail me, and I haven't changed its format since it got me my first job on Wall Street.

First Section (header - centered)

This section should contain your mailing address, mobile telephone number, and email address. You really should include your email address, as this will, in practice, be your primary form of contact with your recruiter and your potential employer.

Second Section (centered)

This section contains your name.

Third Section – Academic Preparation

This is the academic preparation section. List your degrees, the associated colleges and universities, and various specializations; one per line.

Fourth Section – Professional Competencies

This section includes programming languages, operating systems, databases, and other technologies you are familiar with. I like to break up my programming languages into levels of competencies such as *Expert Level*, indicating that I am simply *the man* when it comes to knowing anything and everything about this programming language, and *Working Level*, which means I can code in this about as well as I can code in anything else; I'm not the best in it, but given a few days, a specific task, and access to the internet, I'll muddle my way through.

Fifth Section – Professional Experience

This section contains your previous work experience. If you are still working somewhere while looking for a new job, certainly include your current position. Each entry in my résumé contains the date range of my employment at the firm (month and year), the job title, and the company name. Outline all of your responsibilities and every major project you took on. If you're lacking big projects, include smaller, but significant tasks as well. If you worked with some specific or interesting technology, make sure it's in there as well, as employers will often just skim the text to see if their eyes catch something they recognize.

Sixth Section - Research and Personal Projects

If you have no research work or personal projects (how could you not have personal projects? Didn't you code a simple application or two over the years?), either put some together, or feel free to skip this section entirely. In my résumé, this section includes small software applications and tutorials I released into the wild over the last few years. You can include academic work here as well, as long as it's substantial.

Seventh Section - Publications

Once again, if you happen not to have any publications, skip this section. I post all my published articles in this section. This book is now in there as well.

Eighth Section - Languages

If you speak several languages, sometimes people list them at the bottom of their résumé. Since I speak only English, Russian and barely enough French to be able to ask where the bathroom is before soiling myself, I tend to refrain from including this section on my résumé.

That's all. I do not have a "*References Available Upon Request*" line, as it became clear years ago that it is almost always entirely ignored, and the firms that require references will ask you for them whether this line is on your résumé or not.

Oh, and for those of you who have some strange personal inhibition about having your résumé be more than one page long, stop that right now! I haven't seen a single-page résumé in years, even from interns. My own résumé is four pages long, and no one has yet to complain. There is a good reason why the "*Professional Competencies*" section is on the first page.

So how do you find a programming job on Wall Street?

What I should be asking at this point is *why* do you want to write code for Wall Street, but since you're reading this book, the discussion would probably be fruitless...so here's how you get that Wall Street job.

There are five ways people go about getting jobs in the IT sector on Wall Street - attend a college campus recruiting event, submit your résumé to an online job site, work with a recruiter, get recommended by a friend on the inside, or have the company ask for you by reputation.

Most entry level developers concentrate their efforts on college campus recruiting events, and most experienced developers concentrate their efforts on micro-optimizing their résumés so they would stand out when submitted to various online job search sites.

Well...*most* people think that Africa is a country, so just because *most* people do something, doesn't make it right.

Campus recruiting events

I know I'm going to catch hell for this, but attending a campus recruiting event is probably that worst possible approach to finding work.

There is absolutely nothing to differentiate you from any other first-time-suit-wearing senior. At best, these conferences are nothing more than irritating butt-kissing festivals. At worst, you will begin to think of these circus shows as the standard accepted way of looking for work – leading you to be highly disappointed with the entire process.

Think about the logistics of the event. How can I, as a company representative (that phrase sounds almost dirty), possibly discern anything about you as a candidate after a 15 minutes conversation. The atmosphere is just not conducive for this type of work. After two hours, all the candidates start washing together in my mind, and unless you're so spectacular that I immediately run back to work in order to file your recommendation, there is nothing that will make you stand out from the rest. And if you are good enough to make that strong of an impression in 15 minutes, you don't need me to give you a job on Wall Street...you can probably make a small fortune selling ice at the North Pole.

After the stupidity ends, and I go back to the office, that painstakingly formatted résumé printed on $100 per sheet super-duper 'this-will-most-certainly-get-me-that-job' paper, is about as valuable to me, sitting in a pile, as the 50 electronic copies I get from Monster or CareerBuilder every morning.

Getting recommended by a friend on the inside

I can add nothing of value to this section. If you have a friend on the inside, you either have great luck in life, or you have incredible social skills. I'd argue that for many programmers, the luck factor far outweighs social skills.

Small companies will always prefer to hire on a recommendation of a current employee (in good standing). It's quite difficult to get good candidates (believe me, there aren't that many of them), so if a current employee recommends someone, that candidate will probably get the first shot for the next opening. The reasoning behind this is solid. No one wants to work with an imbecile, and the person giving the recommendation has his reputation on the line...and knows it.

In large banks, if you get hired on the basis of a recommendation from a current employee, that employee stands to receive a relatively fat finder's fee - something around $5,000. This is money well spent for the company - good people are hard to find, and they would have spent much more on a professional recruiter.

The financial arena is not that large, and people shift all the time. Once you have a few years of experience under your belt, you'll find yourself working with the same people from time to time. This can happen when one of you brings the other into the company by recommendation, or if both of you work for separate companies that have a close business relationship. Or even by pure luck; you both just happen to get a job at the same place years after you last worked together. At a certain point, you will have friends in almost every major financial institution on Wall Street (and some outside the financial arena, who may serve as your opportunity for escape, should you ever need one). Don't burn those bridges. You will need these professional contacts as leverage to build your career. Individual careers grow at different paces, and so, one day, you may find your ex-cubicle neighbor in the position of a hiring manager, or as a CEO of his own (already profitable) Wall Street startup. And while some see the world as being balanced and fair, the reality is that the person whom you helped debug that piece of code in the trenches four years ago will think of you before interviewing any new candidates for an open position.

I have close friends – who were all once colleagues – in four NYC-based investment banks, one Chicago based company, and one London based company. I also have standing job offers from a few of these places - not having ever seen or been to any of these companies, but having previously battled through 36-hour coding sessions with each of the guys who are now managers in these firms.

Have the company ask for you

This doesn't happen much with peon coders (I still consider myself to be one of these), but it does occur frequently with management types - even IT management. If you see your progress and inevitable success as being bound to your person, rather than to a company you happen to work for, you eventually begin building a reputation for yourself in some circles. This can happen through a track record of great consulting work, through well-regarded publications, or in some other way, but like in any field, there are superstar recognizable names floating around Wall Street. These guys don't look for jobs. They probably haven't even updated their résumés in years. The companies know them by name, and if they choose to leave their current firm, personalized offers hit their voicemail before they even get the chance to get home. *Come work for us! We've had a private office with your name on the door for months now! Anything you want! Money isn't an issue! Your driver is already waiting outside! We also took the liberty of sending some flowers to your wife for your upcoming anniversary!*

OK. So it's not *that* cliché. The situation is approached in a more tasteful manner, but the intent is the same. This is probably a nice position to be in - I'll let you know if I ever get there (although I'd probably push for a helicopter in favor of a limousine).

Submitting your résumé to an online job site

If you are just starting out, unless you are lucky enough to get recommended by a friend on the inside, this is your only viable option. The goal here is not to find an employer directly - the goal is to find a recruiter - which leads us to...

Working with recruiters

Recruiters (sometimes rather callously referred to as pimps) actively peruse the job board sites. In fact, they are experts at this kind of work. If you want to be cynical about it (and I often do), you can view this as being akin to a jungle cat waiting in hiding for prey.

So how do you approach getting a recruiter...or to be more direct, how do you get a recruiter to find a job for you on Wall Street?

Well, the first part should be obvious. Pad your résumé with *bling* terms (you know the ones), and submit it to any of the popular online job sites. If you have any experience at all, or the right (meaning currently popular) set of technologies under your belt, your approximate wait time should be about...30 minutes. So grab a gallon of coffee, and get ready for the upcoming gauntlet, because once that first email comes in, they will not stop for three days straight. The email and phone calls will eventually trickle down, but I've had recruiters following up on my résumé months after I already accepted a position.

Some years back, when I began a job search through this approach, I set aside an entire day for the task. I woke up in the morning, informed my wife of my plans, and locked myself in the bedroom for the whole day with a laptop. If I was nice enough about it, I'd get slices of pizza pushed under the door every few hours.

If you're silly enough to put your home telephone number on your résumé, tell everyone in the house that the phone is yours for the day. They won't be able to use it anyway.

Once your résumé is submitted, and you have your gallon of coffee next to you, the juggling game begins…

Most recruiters are completely useless (and if you're one of the head-hunters with whom I sometimes have a few beers...feel free to ignore the previous statement...you know I'm right anyway). The vast majority of them know absolutely nothing about technology, and the exhaustive set of their job opportunities consists of the five or six major investment banks in New York - the ones that are *always* hiring.

Eventually, you will learn how to spot them. If you spot them quickly, end the conversation, because, like a used car salesman, if you expose even the smallest sign of interest, they'll chew your ear off for the rest of the day. Don't waste your time with them - they won't give you the leverage you need. What they will do is keep you on the phone for hours, asking you to explain what a 'virtual method' is, because someone gave them the answer at some point, and they use that to blindly filter résumés.

I hang up on these guys...waste of time...they will never understand what you want from a job anyway.

The recruiters you *do* want are the seasoned veterans who have direct contacts with hiring managers, CTOs and HR personnel. These guys, you will also learn to recognize, and they will provide you with opportunities that no-one else has. There are companies that work with only one recruiter, and that recruiter will be the only one who has access to the job opportunities in that firm...and he is your man.

Filter out the crap, and find the guy you trust. Then, keep him! Keep him for as long as he's willing to work with you. Take him to lunch. Buy flowers for his wife. Ask about his kids. Trusted 'pimps' are very, very rare...like a trusted car mechanic. If you're lucky enough to find a guy you trust – one who doesn't make you feel like he's selling you a used car – do everything you can to maintain that relationship. Part of this means that the next time you're seeking work, give him the first shot at finding you a job. If he's worth his salt, he'll ask you what you want - you know, the important things *other* than money, like location, company size, project type, etc – and he'll actually take everything into consideration when looking for a position for you. The good guys are not interested in a quick commission score. They build their reputations by listening to exactly what each company needs from an employee, and exactly what each employee needs from a company, and they do their best to make a match without forcing either side.

The trick to getting through this day of recruiter-juggling is to filter out the headhunters so that *you* don't get screwed later on.

Let me explain...

Recruiters make money by taking a referral fee from the company when they find a matching candidate. The recruiter will typically only get paid if the new hire remains at the company for some minimum amount of time - usually three months. These referral fees often correlate with the negotiated salary, and can be very, very large. For candidates who pull off $200,000 salaries, the recruiter can make the kind of money that will make you want to rethink programming as a career choice.

That being said, the companies that don't work with a just one recruiter exclusively (mostly large investment banks), will only accept your résumé from one of them - the *first* one. If you are contacted by several headhunters, all promising you a job at International Bank X, give permission to send your résumé to only *one* of them. If the company is interested in you, and they later find out that your résumé was submitted by several recruiters because you didn't keep track of them, they will drop your butt on the floor. They do not want the legal hassle involved in figuring out which recruiter earned the referral fee. They would rather not talk to you at all than get involved in a dispute of this kind.

...and so we come full circle...

If only one recruiter is allowed to submit your résumé to a company, make sure it's the guy who knows the CTO or the hiring manager, rather than the novice who will submit you into the generic résumé pool.

Once you get the interview and reach the offer stage, a good recruiter can be fully expected to take the reigns during salary negotiation. If you're not the type who likes to talk about money with your potential employer, let the recruiter handle it. Chances are, he will get you 15% over what you expected (or asked for). He makes his living doing this. The company knows this. The last thing the recruiter wants to do is blow the deal at this stage of the game, so don't be afraid of him botching up the job. If the company is not flexible, the recruiter will tell you their best and final offer without creating an uncomfortable situation between you and your future employer. If the company is flexible, and you are a better candidate than they've come across prior to you showing up, the recruiter will handle the situation in a more than appropriate manner...and you will probably be pleasantly surprised.

I have only one recruiter. I've worked with him for years. He maintains a very small and exclusive client list. He knows the kind of companies I like, the kind of work I prefer to do, and he is familiar enough with my technical abilities without having to ask for them every time I am in need of his services. I don't bother posting my résumé anywhere online (which doesn't stop some of the newbie headhunters from constantly following up with me on my 3-year old résumé). My average turnaround time between leaving one place and being given an offer from my next employer is twelve days.

The Wall Street job interview

For some reason, outsiders seem to think that the Wall Street job interview is somehow fundamentally different from all other IT job interviews. This may be true if you are interviewing for a spot where deep knowledge of financial markets or instruments is required, but since I've already gone over the fact that no-one will expect anything of the kind from you on your first interview at a Wall Street firm, you might as well put that fear out of your head and believe me when I tell you that there is no fundamental difference, at this stage, between interviewing for a programming position on Wall Street and interviewing for a programming position in any other IT sector.

58 – So You Want To Be A Wall Street Programmer?

I've interviewed dozens of people for programming jobs over the years, for various firms - both large investment banks and small hedge funds - and while I can't speak for any of my colleagues, I will do my best to describe to you exactly what I look for in a candidate. I am inclined to believe that most experienced developers tend to look for the same things that I do, but since interviewing is far from being a science (there really is *no* method to the madness in this case – ask the guy who turned me down at the beginning of my career because he couldn't find a parking spot that morning, and was irritable the whole day), the person interviewing you may have a completely different set of values.

At the end of this section, in an attempt to bring more practical goodness to the book, I will list some of the questions I often ask at interviews, as well as some of the questions that have been asked of me.

One factor in a candidate's résumé that is absolutely of no concern to me is the school. This applies both to school name and choice of major.

I choose to ignore the academic background of the candidate simply because over the years, I failed to find any evidence supporting the fact that an academic background in Computer Science has any direct benefit on the skill set or overall performance of a programmer. You will see that many terrific developers joined the ranks of Wall Street programmers with backgrounds in physics, chemistry, mathematics, philosophy and even art.

I also rarely look at the school name. When I do, it's only in the hopes that it might freshen up what has, up to that point, been a rather lackluster conversation. I completed my undergraduate degree at a city college, but received my masters from an Ivy League university. To this day I assert that I received a better education from the city college - both in the foundational theory of computer science, and in practical skills. To bring my point home, let me just mention that the best developer I've ever worked with was self-taught, and had no formal education above high-school.

People who are new to interviewing others folks, feel that they have to bring a barrage of questions to the table. Their approach is to bombard the candidate with increasingly harder questions until the candidate breaks.

This is both foolish and selfish.

This kind of approach has no purpose - it tells you nothing about the candidate aside from pure technical skills, which should never be the highest priority on your list. The goal, simply, should be to ascertain whether you, as a developer, would be willing to work with this person.

By using the question blitz approach (or even worse, the "*How do you move Mount Fuji*" type of questions), all you're doing is stroking your own ego.

When I interview a candidate - entry level or otherwise - the most important thing I look for is his ability to hold a conversation.

I do throw in a technical question or two, but those exist purely to reflect the specific technical requirements of the job at hand, and to filter out the few extremely incompatible candidates who managed to have slipped through the initial résumé check.

The best kind of interview - one which consistently results in building extremely compatible and effective development teams - is when a formal interview "degenerates" into a conversation between two geeks.

I want the candidate who is able to have a conversation about programming style, the benefits of choosing one technology over another, his choice of programming editors, his thoughts on any recent technological fad, or even a discussion of why some technology presented in a popular science fiction television show would be impossible in real life.

I want the candidate to be familiar with things like Dr. Dobbs Journal,

Slashdot, and have a list of personal favorite blogs.

I want the person I would be working with to be able to relate to me and my team, not only at the C++ level, but at a social level. The various jokes and geeky references floating around the office should never go over anyone's head.

In a nutshell, you should be comfortable with the culture, and while most certainly, you will not be rejected if you've been living in a cave for the past decade reading programming books, your life at the office, surrounded by geeks, will be much more fun if you can quote at least one line from Office Space (that would be great.)

The 'best developer I ever worked with' whom I mentioned before? He interviewed me for my second job on Wall Street. Some time later, he admitted that the only reason I stood out from all other candidates was because I had a full-blown argument with him in the interview room over some nonsense feature in the **gdb** debugger. Some wouldn't consider it smart to argue with folks who are interviewing you, but to him, this showed that I had an interest in the culture, was willing to argue over something I considered to be right, had an ability to present my case in an intelligent manner, and, probably least of all, that I've had some experience with the **gdb** debugger. I had an offer from that company waiting in my voicemail before I even reached the ground floor of the building on my way out.

But I won't keep you any longer. As promised, here are some questions that I tend to ask on programming interviews. Some of these, I admit, were originally questions that were asked of me at one point.

What do you do if you have a situation where a bug shows up during normal execution, but turns out to be impossible to reproduce when running under a debugger, or when attempting to isolate it by inserting extra debug output?

Such bugs are sometimes referred to as "Heisenbugs"; meaning that any attempt to study or observe them changes their behavior. Please understand that no matter what answer you give, I, as the interviewer, can always augment the question to nullify your response. I'm looking for two things here: your ability to bring reason to a problem, and, hopefully, your eventual admission that sometimes you have to put all those nice toys away, and just eyeball the code to find the problem. All too often, people use tools as crutches unnecessarily.

What could be the cause of the problem when a process dumps core and prints out the message "pure virtual function called"?

This often happens on Solaris machines – but that's not very important. What *is* important, is for me to get a glimpse into your thought process as you mull over the problem. How can a pure virtual function be called in a running process? Shouldn't the compiler catch any such attempts before you even build the thing? Well, there are multiple causes for this, but I will be really, really happy if your thought process leads you to explore the possibility of a multi-threaded process, where a destructor is called on an object in one thread, and another thread calls a method on the parent class of something in the midst of being destroyed. Fun stuff, that C++, isn't it?

You've just accepted a position at a company. One of your duties is to manage the support lines for a few hours a day, and it just so happens that a trader calls up screaming about a problem while everyone else is out of the office. You're still new, and don't know anything about the problem. You can't reach anyone by cell phone or any other method, and the trader is getting more and more impatient. What do you do?

There's no right answer to this. If you insist that there is, you're either fooling yourself, or you're just lying. There's no right answer to any such situational questions, as I can always change the parameters of the question. The goal is the same – I want to get a glimpse of your thought process.

Incidentally, this question was asked of me during one of my first interviews, and after a few minutes of bouncing the ball back and forth, the only thing I could think of was telling the trader to fuck off. This was probably what the interviewer wanted to hear from me anyway, as a few weeks after I joined the firm, I think I heard that exact response coming from him when talking to an angry trader on the phone. I don't recommend using this as an answer if you want the position – the trader was just trying to do his job, and it's probably your software that's causing the problem. But alas, my answer on that interview was of a more conventional kind.

*Assume you have a class with 100 integer members. Would it be safe to do a **memset()** on the object in order to quickly zero out the memory?*

Everyone answers '**no**'. Of course they do...the question is phrased in such a way that you *feel* the answer should be '**no**'. And it is. But *why* is the answer '**no**'? This one isn't situational. I really want the correct answer. Specifically, I want to find out if you're aware of the existence of **virtual tables** and **vtable** pointers – and the understanding, that at some point, someone might want to derive something from this class, and bring one of these **vtable** pointers into existence without realizing that there is a ***memset()*** hiding somewhere in the calling code.

When would you need a virtual destructor? (and if answered correctly, why wouldn't you always use a virtual destructor?)

I never asked this silly question, until I began noticing that many programmers lack a fundamental understanding of the issues involved. Same deal as with the **memset()** question above – I want to see if you understand the concept of **virtual**. You claim to know C++, so I fully expect you to understand the language's most fundamental concept. Yes, you will leak memory if you leave it out and delete an object through a parent pointer. Yes, space is still at a premium, and yes, the virtual table pointer takes up unnecessary space if it's not needed.

Reverse a character string.

This is a rather commonplace question, but I like it. You'd be surprised how many people can't answer this one. I blame it on the fact that colleges no longer cover pointers, and prefer to focus on higher-level languages. There is no getting away from pointers, and so, I always throw this or a similar question on the table.

Here are a few more mundane questions I ask when I simply want to test a candidate's technical skills:

Write a one-liner to check if a number is a power of two.

When must you use an initialization list?
Why is the parameter to a copy constructor passed by reference?
Explain virtual inheritance.
Why shouldn't you throw an exception inside a destructor?
*Why would you use the **volatile** qualifier?*
*Why would you use the **explicit** qualifier?*
*What can the statement **delete this** in a destructor be harmful?*
*Why is it a bad idea to write **using namespace ...** in a header file?*
How can you access command line arguments inside the code?
How can you access environment variables inside the code?
*Explain the concept of **Copy on Write**.*

Oh. If you show up in my office looking for a job, and during the interview it becomes obvious that you know the answer to every one of these questions because you read this book…well…I'll hire you.

Fear of the code

The following is for entry level developers. Experienced developers...go grab some coffee and come back in five minutes.

I see this time and time again…

A young developer joins a company either straight out of school or coming out of his first job. His strongest emotion is fear. This is understandable, and is generally accepted. After all, he has much to be afraid of. First and foremost, there is the fear of not making a good first impression (whatever the consequences of that may be). Second, there is the fear of getting fired - for whatever reasons - the consequence of which is usually the acceptance of another position in another firm...leading to the same exact situation. And third, there is fear of the code.

This third fear is not addressed in any job search or interview guide. It also happens to be the most irrational thing I consistently come across.

Fear of the code is fear of breaking the norm. It is loosely bound to both the fear of not making a good impression (of not 'fitting in'), and to the fear of getting fired.

Given the first assignment, the new developer is extremely hesitant about making code changes. Because he is afraid of breaking the 'norm', he strives to do everything within his power to find patterns to follow within the existing code. This same developer was probably a superstar coder until this moment, but has now mentally reverted to the ranks of an amateur - not fit to deal with anything that might justify the salary he just negotiated with HR.

Some senior developers advocate doing this sort of thing; falling into a firm-accepted development pattern. And this is good advice for a seasoned programmer, in the context where he already knows the impact of his potential changes and the circumstances surrounding the code base. But such advice can be detrimental to a new developer.

It would be of benefit to you, the new developer, to realize that this fear doesn't only manifest itself inside your head. The behavior is noticeable, and makes you look...well...weak. The less experienced middle-managers and their immediate (but still green) superiors might take advantage of such weakness by pulling rank. It's natural human behavior to form an intuitive order of dominance, and if the new developer does not - for lack of a better euphemism - grow a pair, and pull out of that state sooner rather than later, his time at the firm might not be as pleasant as it could have been.

The intuitive strategy of following the norm and playing it safe does not work in the context of a small company. Here, when I make a hiring decision, there are two things I want from the new developer; learn fast, and don't break anything.

Once the context switches from a smaller company to a larger one, the second requirement disappears. In larger firms, such as investment banks, there are entire frameworks in place to prevent one from doing things like *rm -rf **, or locking up production databases. But even in a small firm, nothing is irreversible, and while it's important to me that the developer doesn't break anything, it's not out of fearing production consequences, it's more out of my desire to not feel that I made a mistake in my hiring judgments.

Incidentally, fear of the code is not limited to code alone, but extends equally to other matters at the office. The fear manifests itself in internal questions such as *'When does everyone usually go home? It's 5:30 already. Can I go home or will they think I'm lazy?"*, and *"Who can or can't I CC on this email? Does the CTO need to be bothered with this?"* The result is extremely timid behavior for the duration of time it takes to become more comfortable with the environment.

The trick is to keep breathing...

Do what your brilliance was brought on to do: write code to the best of your ability. Write code with your characteristics. Write code with your own input. Write code with your original insight.

Salary and bonuses

Admit it - this is the only reason you're reading this book.

Wall Street salaries, comparatively speaking, are among the highest in the world. This, of course, does not pertain only to programmers, but it most certainly doesn't exclude them.

At this point, I feel compelled to mention that if you did not read the self-hedging disclaimer at the beginning of the book, you might find that doing so would be of some benefit prior to reading this section.

72 – So You Want To Be A Wall Street Programmer?

If you're just not of the type to read disclaimers (an odd character trait if there ever was one), the summary is this: take everything you read with a grain of salt, and you'll be better off.

Let's move on...

An entry-level developer holding a recent undergraduate degree can expect to pull in somewhere around 50k per year as a starting salary. If you're writing code (either at the application or infrastructure level), and your salary is less than 40k, you're getting ripped off. If, as an entry-level hacker, your salary is over 80k, ma-zel tov, you'll hit the salary ceiling sooner than you think. At this point in your career, there is little variance in salary with respect to general job description, company size, company focus, or even school name.

If you stay with the same company for an extended period of time, you can expect to make somewhere around 100k within five years. You will still be sitting in a cubicle at this point, but now you'll be able to afford a good MP3 player, and any other tech toys to make you happy. You'll also probably be married by this time, and begin to sadly realize that 100k can't buy much in New York City - least of all, a house.

If you live in Manhattan, a 600 square foot apartment - basically a closet - will go for around 2k a month (depending on which part of

Manhattan you decide to live in). This will give you a commute of 15 minutes, but will seriously dig into your savings. If you live in the outer boroughs (Brooklyn, Queens, etc...), your rent will be much cheaper, but your commute will increase to 90 minutes each way.

If you're not the type to stay in one company for a long time, you'll notice that your salary jumps at a higher rate as compared to the salary of your friends who are still working at that first firm. This is mostly a side effect of the way recruiters work. You will typically find that during your first few years on Wall Street, having a good recruiter will yield you about 15k more with each job switch.

So should you just hop around from job to job until your mattress is so stuffed with money that you need a ladder to go to bed at night?

Well...during the boom of the late nineties, this is exactly what most consultants did; they joined a firm for six months, only to use the new experience as leverage to get a better paying position for the next few months.

This doesn't last. It *is* a good idea to get a solid breadth of experience as your career is growing, and refraining from staying at one place for too long is one of the better ways of doing this, but the salary hops stop pretty quickly. Eventually, your base salary will exceed your experience level and you will either start making side jumps, in terms of compensation, or you will have to take a salary cut in order to center yourself in the food chain.

Another reason you might want to remain in one place for an extended period of time (as many do in large investment banks), is the bonus.

You will have no comprehension of what a real bonus is until you stay put for a few years. Folks who stick around for 5 or 10 years in a large investment bank eventually begin to use their salaries for coffee money, and base their living budgets on bonuses alone. Why not? If you're doing a good job after 7 years - passable, not even exemplary - your bonus might be something along the lines of 100% of your salary.

But it takes guts to base your family budget on a yet-to-be-seen bonus. Bonuses are *not* guaranteed. It doesn't matter what people outside of the company, people inside different groups of your company, or even what your recruiter tells you. Unless it's well defined in your contract and there is a mutual understanding between you and the human resources person you dealt with, there is *no* guarantee of a bonus. This is because bonuses are *not* compensation; they are *motivation*, and companies are not under any obligation to give them out, although it usually makes good strategic business sense to do so.

Now, all of this is for IT folks. Traders and business guys are under a completely different dynamic when it comes to bonuses. Traders typically live by the bonus (with a mediocre base salary). For them, the yearly bonus can be in the millions, and is highly tied to performance. As a developer working for a few years in one company, your bonus is also bound to performance, but typically ranges from 10% to 50% of your salary. If you have a bad year, you'll forgo that big screen TV you wanted to buy. If a trader has a bad year - or a *really* bad few minutes - he will no longer be able to send his eldest to college.

Let me restate something...

Bonuses are *not* in the same camp as salary, and it would be to your advantage to refrain from coupling the two in your mind. Salary is negotiated, predetermined, and expected. Bonuses are not seen as any of these things by the folks giving them out. In fact, more often than not, the big wigs upstairs who determine your bonus are not the same people who handle your salary. Salary is determined by a combination of human resources grunts, the people at the desk of the CFO, some set of managers many layers above you, and, to some extent, the shareholders. Bonuses are determined by a group of people who are trained in employee motivation, with some input from traders who know you, your direct manager, and the occasional performance review. Bonuses are given out to retain people. They are given out to keep people from walking out the door after the drunken stupor of the company Christmas party wears off, and they begin thinking about improving their situation for the upcoming year.

But even though bonuses are just motivation and should be treated as such, people around the world look onto Wall Street with dollar signs in their eyes after hearing about the bonuses. Even though they are just motivation, the human resources lady at your next interview will ask you about your bonus levels at the last few companies so that she can take it into account when determining your salary. And even though they are just motivation, the IRS doesn't care, and will happily tax any bonus you get at something close to 50%.

Speaking of expectations...

There was a story recently bouncing around the airwaves claiming that a big name New York City based investment bank had managed to pull off its most profitable quarter ever, and this guaranteed a bonus of $500,000 for each employee.

What utter nonsense…

Even if the earnings were as much as reported, the firm in question has over 20,000 employees, and the bonuses are not partitioned equally. By the time the top dogs get their share, the grunts will be lucky to get enough to cover their next Starbucks run. This is an exaggeration, of course, but you get the point.

Personally, I do not rely on bonuses. Never have, never will. I say this to every recruiter I ever worked with. Total compensation (base salary + bonus) means nothing to me. As far as financial motivation, choose your jobs based on base salary alone. You don't know how long you're going to stay at the company. You don't know if you will qualify for the bonus if you do stay a year or more. You don't know if the company will go under within a few months. You don't know if the instruments they use to hedge most of their holdings will plummet in value because of some unexpected international event. You don't know many, many things when it comes to bonuses.

I would not base the health and comfort of my family on so many unknowns. If you get a good bonus, take your family on vacation, or buy that big screen TV - consider it a gift (one that's taxed at 50%). If traders can live by the bonus, that's fine. They are probably more comfortable with such a dynamic. After all, hedging risk is their job - it's in their blood. A programmer's job is to maintain stability and predictability, and so, you really shouldn't get too comfortable with the promise of bonuses.

Incidentally, the saddest bonus I've ever received (aside from not receiving one at all, that is), is a pair of half-rusty metal cufflinks. I don't even own any shirts that use cufflinks. Even a Hallmark card would have been better, but I guess Hallmark doesn't make "*The Company is Broke*" cards.

So you code, and you code, and some years pass...so where are you now?

Senior developers and technical leads tend to make more money (duh!), but they are usually working as independent consultants at this point. Consultants who are able to market themselves as one-person do-it-all solution machines are very well off - but you can really only pull that off after you gain a few years of experience. Consultants are typically not eligible for bonuses - they set their own hourly, monthly or quarterly rates.

The senior developers and project leads who don't work as independent consultants make most of their money from bonuses as well. Their base salaries range from 150k (way underpaid) to around 300k (probably overpaid).

From 9 to 5?

The days of coming to work at 9 and leaving by 5 are long gone. When I first began working on Wall Street, I was eager to make something of myself and my career, and thus spent long hours at the office in an attempt to make a good impression. We were newlyweds at the time, so suffice it to say, my wife wasn't pleased.

But it seemed as if it was necessary. We had just moved into our first apartment together, and the realization that I was now responsible for supporting two people (my wife was still finishing her degree), paying rent, and all the bills, by myself, was frightening.

I was earning $50k at the time, but seeing me work, you'd have thought I was getting a portion of the company's profits. We were all the same way back then - the company hired four or five young kids out of college around the same time, and we were all learning the ropes together, so to speak.

I was responsible for writing the interfaces for the various exchanges in which the company did business. The company traded options and hedged them with futures. This was the equity world, which in retrospect seems a whole lot easier to deal with than the fixed income sector I've been focusing on as of late.

About mid-way into my tenure at the firm, another young developer left the company and took a position at the country's largest ISP at the time - you know the one (it was before broadband). The project she was working on was left half-done (if that), and I got the task of finishing up the leftovers.

The interface she was working on dealt with the ASX exchange in Australia, which doesn't exactly fit into New York's time zone. I remember having to gradually come into the office later and later in order to synchronize with the Sydney office hours. I needed the support of the ASX technical team, and email wasn't always the best or easiest option. At the peak of development, I was working from 1 PM to midnight. By the time the interface was released, I wasn't in the best physical condition - the time shifting had taken its toll. But it wasn't over yet.

After the first full trading day, strange errors began popping up in the software. Log files weren't much help, and one night I found myself being woken up at 3 AM and having to fetch a cab to go to the office in order to diagnose the problem. It turned out to be a one character change (from an 'L' to an 'H', if I recall correctly) in a configuration file, but by the time the issue was resolved, it didn't make much sense to go back home.

At one point during the development/debug phase of the project, I stayed at the office for 36 hours straight, at the end of which I was finally forced to go home for a break (my suspicions are that the real reason behind this was that I was starting to smell). If I go back to that office now, I bet I can still find the military-style cot I slept on for a few hours during this adventure.

This might have been an extreme situation, but I've spoken with a few experienced developers since, who have admitted that they've been in similar (and worse!) situations when they first started out.

One thing to note is that no one at the company asked me to work such long hours. My wife certainly wasn't pleased with the situation. It was my choice. Something in my own head made me believe that this was the right way.

Things have changed - but not much.

My average work day now is from 7:30 AM to 6:00 PM. Sometimes, if the situation demands it, I also work from home after leaving the office. This is no longer an extreme situation. Many folks spend more time at the office than I do. A few spend less, but 10-12 hours per day seems to be the norm around here. My wife, who now works as a quantitative analyst for a small hedge-fund, works about 12 hours a day. She sometimes works from home at night as well.

It isn't easy. Many people burn out really quickly. It could certainly be attributed to the New York City culture. My IT friends on the west coast laugh at me when I tell them how much time my wife and I spend at the office.

Office characters

Stereotypical personalities are abound in every profession, and while most folks believe that programmers typically fall into the unshaven, Star Trek watching, Frodo obsessed, glasses-wearing, geek category, nothing can be further from the truth. We are, in fact, many different shades of unshaven, Star Trek watching, Frodo obsessed, glasses-wearing geeks.

But while geeks we may all be, there are always variations in personality types. There are 'templates' of people who often serve as either 'the reason I'm still working here after 5 years', or as 'the reason I stormed out of that place four days short of receiving my bonus'. Here are some of the personality types you'll come across while hacking code on Wall Street.

The burned-out developer

Oh boy. Even as you make your first steps into the offices of your first employer on Wall Street, rest assured that you are no more than five years away from becoming this guy. This happens in every area of software development, not just Wall Street. I'm pretty certain it happens in other professional fields as well, but I can't vouch for that. If you're an experienced developer, I'm sure I don't need to describe to you the typical burned-out coder. Nor do I need to describe him if you're fresh out of school...believe me, you'll know him when you see him. And when you do see him, you will actually feel physical pain when you realize the miserable state that he sees himself in.

There are various causes for this. Personality might have something to do with it. Dissatisfaction with the current firm is certainly a factor. A timely midlife crisis might also be the culprit. But usually, it's the belief that after years in the business he earns less respect than that greenie that just shuffled through the door for his first day of work. Job hopping seems to help, but it's not a solution, it just holds off the depression for a bit while you're settling in.

Many developers at this stage throw caution to the wind and start their own one-man software shops. Do a search for 'MicroISV', and you'll see what I'm talking about. Some MicroISV owners do quite well for themselves. You can do worse as a software developer than risking it all in the hopes of being able to use your skills to support yourself without having a pointy-haired boss. In fact, some will argue that having a pointy-haired boss is much worse - no matter the pay.

If you're an entry-level developer, don't be afraid of asking the burned-out developers for help. Their issues are not with you. They are typically loaded with experience, and are willing to help you out if needed (you might have to listen to a few depressing monologues though).

The manager wannabe

I can't even count how many places I've left because of these guys...

If you've watched the (brilliant) BBC television series 'The Office', you'll immediately recognize Gareth as being exactly the type of guy I am referring to. I believe the character's name is Dwight in the far less brilliant American version of the show. For our purpose, let's call this guy Bob. Bob is about two or three years out of college, and while he has not yet reached official manager status, Bob has managed to dig himself into a place where he is given a bit of power over a few people 'below' him. From my experience, this inevitably turns into a situation that will make you run out to the nearest book store to buy a copy of Animal Farm and begin making situational comparisons. Power corrupts. Orwell would be proud.

What makes Bob dangerous (especially if you are one of those poor schmucks 'below' him), is that he is far from being an idiot. While making sure that those who put him into his present position see him in the best light possible, he rains down hell on those in his care. Bob's first order of business is to purchase every book known to man on the topic of effective people management. You'll know this when terms like "critical path" and "thinking outside the box" start coming out of his mouth. If there is one thing Bob knows how to do, it's getting himself into higher and higher positions of management - usually while leaving everyone behind him with a bad aftertaste.

I'm afraid that if, at this point, you are 'below' Bob, you can't do much about the situation (aside from quitting of course...and you'll probably be better off). It's not easy to stand up to people like Bob because as a relatively new developer, it will most likely be seen as an unprofessional act on your part, and you will probably be branded as 'not being a team player'.

In my own professional career, I've had more than one confrontation with various Bobs, but only once did I wield enough leverage to have the guy fired (and it was a fine day indeed).

The 'work-is-just-work' guy

I've met only a few of these characters in my career, but they surely had an effect on my perspective of work, and life in general. Professionally, they have forgotten more about programming than you have ever known, are able to put together a flawless system from scratch with superhuman speed, without ever asking for help from anyone, and are able to hold their own in any conversation concerning both modern and obsolete technology.

After punch-out time, the 'work-is-just-work' guy plays his guitar, rides his motorcycle, spends quality time with his children, cooks dinner for his family, and volunteers for charity organizations. But never does he touch a computer on his time away from work. He might not even *own* a computer. He certainly doesn't have any computer magazines lying around the house, and his bookshelves have never seen a book covering topics that include curly brackets (or braces, if you prefer).

And yet, he gained his knowledge from somewhere. I honestly have no explanation for this. If you question him, his nonchalance will convince you that life over vocation is the only sane path to follow. He may be right. I consider myself to be a competent technologist, but I have three rooms filled to the ceiling with computer books, and in one corner, is a guitar that I never learned how to play.

The old-school über-coder

If you're an entry level coder just out of school, this is the guy you will start wishing would take you under his wing. Let's call him Kevin - because that was the name of my old-school über-coder (and my first CTO) when I was fresh out of college. Experienced developers, while still able to notice people like Kevin, are no longer as impressed or intimidated. But you, newbie, will stare wide-eyed as Kevin pulls UNIX commands out of thin air that you've never heard of, combines them with pipes and redirection with speed and grace that will make you crave a cigarette, resulting in code that does more as a script hacked together in 5 minutes than your entire graduating class, pulling together years of academic-fueled, object-oriented, design-pattern-laced, Java knowledge could ever dream of doing.

It will be years before you come to the realization that while you were sitting there, aspiring to be like him, he was aspiring to be you again -

to sit in his corner and code quietly with his headphones on, instead of sitting in meetings all day long, cursing everyone under his nose and wishing that they would all just leave him alone.

The faker

As another reference to a television character, this is Wall Street's version of George Costanza - so let's call him George. George has an immaculate résumé filled with years of prestigious roles. He applies for project management positions (claiming that all those pesky coding details are far behind him), and shines at the interview - seemingly filled with general knowledge of all financial and IT related topics.

There is only one problem...he doesn't know anything.

Oh sure, at one point, George might have taken a class in Excel, perhaps even Pascal. And he might have spent the early part of his career hacking code (poorly). But what George really excels at, is self-promotion. It isn't hard to pass a Wall Street interview when the potential employer is really in need, and specific, technical knowledge is not high on the priority list for the job at hand.

The problems arise when George has to actually do something. A project manager, while perhaps not the most practically technical job in the IT sector, is still expected to understand the requirements of a trading system and the capabilities and limitations of the individual developers working on it. More importantly, he should have at least some understanding of how long certain phases of development should take, if not how long a certain module would take to develop given the requirements, the technology used, and the ability and experience of the developer assigned to the task.

George has none of these skills, but the skills he does possess are - unfortunately for you - excellent in allowing him to keep a hold on his cushy position (mostly through golf-games and frequent buddy-lunches with the upper management). So what does George do on a day-to-day basis? Well, just like George Costanza, he puts on a perpetual face of annoyance to seem busy to people who pass him by, and occasionally throws a generic remark on the table during a meeting.

The developer who isn't

This is more Wall Street centric. It's accepted as a truth on Wall Street that folks in the trading, financial, and business areas of the company typically get more money (and usually respect) than the average developer. In fact, developers are mostly seen as a necessary evil - sometimes a liability - but more on this later.

As a result, a lot of mediocre developers that write code on Wall Street are there because they were, frankly, too dumb to get the necessary credentials in order to get into the finance or business areas. So they learned Java (usually in 24 hours), and began hitting keys in a cubicle at an investment bank with the aspiration that perhaps the proximity will somehow give then the leverage they need to get to do what they really want to do.

The truth is that it's quite easy to take the business route in a large company, especially since most of them provide official channels for doing so. Combine this with the fact that the business path usually leads to greener pastures than the technological alternative, and you'll find that many people do spend all of their time as 'programmers' learning the business side of things, losing all of their technological skills in the process and probably alienating a few people along the way. If you ask me - and I guess, in a way, you are - there is a certain sadness in this, as well as a certain logic. After a few years, the only people left hacking code are the ones who truly want to hack code.

Wall Street traders

One of the things you quickly learn in any programming domain is to identify who your customers are. If you write code on Wall Street, overwhelmingly, your customers are traders.

Now, this may be a tad obvious, but everything I write in this book, and especially in this section, comes from my own experience. Your perspective on traders may be drastically different from my own. But after years of conversations with different hacker colleagues, it seems that my viewpoint is not that much off center.

In all my years of programming on Wall Street, I have never been able to get through a comfortable conversation with a trader. Not one. Not ever. Not in any context. Not in a bar while relatively sober during a company outing. Not in a bar while fully drunk during a personal outing. Not at the canteen. Not even at the urinals.

Part of it, I think, is that many programmers - myself included - are introverts. The thing developers call a 'programming zone', that state of mind akin to a writer's trance, where everything is going just right, your productivity seems to increase tenfold, you're completely centered, and ideas (or code) are flowing from your head faster than your hands can deal with them, requires a certain love for solitude. Most traders, however, are social extroverts. They spend hours on the phone with clients and brokers, chatting up a storm, laughing, joking, making deals, screaming at various people when the need arises, and occasionally screaming at the television mounted on the wall when a basketball game is on. I'm not implying that there is anything wrong with this. It's just that this level of energy is a few levels higher than what I'm comfortable with, and so, close, honest conversations with traders tend to suffer as a result.

In all honesty, sometimes it feels like a school playground where the popular jocks are overwhelmingly intimidating in the eyes of a geek. Even younger traders can make me feel like a child at times - simply because they're so good at getting their point across in a vibrant, energetic, confident manner - where as I would tend to slow down a conversation to ponder over some point.

Any traders reading this? Let's have lunch. I'll trade you a free beer for an honest answer.

The question?

What the hell do you do all day?

I really want to know.

Yes, I know the generalities, and I know the technical background of it all, but I want to know the mundane details as well. What is the thought-pattern as you scour the market for a good deal? How does the strategy form in your head? Is it all mechanical and numeric, or do the best traders have some sort of a visual relationship layout in their head for forming good trades? Is there fear in not getting a good bonus? Is it a nonsense fear, as in *"I won't be able to get a nicer car this year"*, or is it a real fear like *"I won't be able to pay for my child's next semester in school"*?

I'll buy you two beers if you manage to turn off the extrovert and tell me the honest story of your first day as a trader.

The programmer-trader relationship is stronger than that of a shrink-wrapped application developer and some customer in a computer store.

First, we sit close together - everyday. If you work for a few years on Wall Street as a programmer, you're almost guaranteed to spend some time on the trading floor - either doing support (not fun), or actually writing code in the same physical space where traders are doing their work, simply because the company is just that small.

Second, we feed each other's families.

If there was ever a symbiotic relationship, it is one between programmers and traders on Wall Street. In very simple terms, they cannot do their jobs without our software, and we do not get paid without them using the software. What surprises many developers starting out on Wall Street, is that, as customers, traders don't actually want out product. In fact, nothing would make a trader happier than if we took our software and just disappeared.

The logic stems from the way a trader works. A good trader enters a state not unlike a programmer's zone or a writer's trance. The difference is that they are able to sustain it for longer periods of time than the typical 2 or 3 hours we're capable of. The mental coordination is a thing of wonder that I find myself sometimes envious of. Where we are able to hurdle across orders of magnitude in code; jumping from the micro-optimization of a single function to thinking about the overall abstract design of the entire system, a trader is capable of leveraging a strategy that needs to balance various instruments hedged across a multitude of other instruments, across multiple sectors, across multiple exchanges, across multiple portfolios - sometimes in a matter of a few seconds.

And yet...they don't want our software.

The very same product we create for them to be able to do their job is a nuisance at best, and a hindrance at worst. It may be an absolute necessity, but it's often treated with much disdain. The 3 millisecond delay imposed by anything within the code is a hindrance. The cool new feature you're proud of which required moving the "SEND" button 5 pixels to the left, is a hindrance. Consistency and speed are of supreme importance, and this is just not the way of a programmer who is always looking for ways to improve the software. All a trader wants is to be able to execute a trade when they know is should be executed. Nothing, absolutely *nothing* in the code should change their mental perception of the way the game is to be played. Any such change in this mental perception is treated as a road block; making them less effective in the market place...the same market place where they put their reputations...the same market place where they put their money...the same market place where they earn money to feed their children.

It may be a grid of rows and columns containing option strikes and calculations for us, but it's a living, evolving battlefield for the traders, and they don't need you messing with it.

You don't need to have honest, meaningful conversations with them if you don't want to, but if you understand where the traders are coming from, you'll be that much stronger as a developer on Wall Street.

Traders fully believe they can do the job of the programmer. After a while, programmers fully believe they can do the job of the trader. You can't. They can't. Accept it and move on.

There are a few developers who manage to put enough time and effort into their careers to rise to a level where they are just as proficient in trading as they are in building trading systems. These guys are amazing to watch. They also tend to pull off a lot of money - obviously. Personally, this requires a level of interest in financial markets that I just don't have. It would be nice to be "The Man", but I'm just not that motivated.

On a, perhaps more entertaining but practically useless, note, traders and programmers could not be more physically different. If you ever visit an investment bank, and are presented with two floors where people sit and stare at computer screens, you will immediately know which floor is the trading floor, and which is the IT department. All the traders I've ever worked with were clean-shaven, very well built, had rather expensive looking haircuts and all seemed to be above average in height. If they begin losing their hair, they often shave the entire head. They care about their looks. This is just their world.

I, on the other hand, consider myself lucky if I remember to put on pants in the morning before showing up to work. This is where being married helps. And if I forget to shave for a few days, I am guaranteed to be the only sasquatch on the trading floor (a convenient way to spot a programmer on support duty).

As far as physical build, for some traders this may be a matter of necessity rather than of vanity. If you're trading in the pit, at certain times of the day, it helps to be able to outmaneuver the other guy in order to get someone's attention to pull off a good trade. If you've never visited the nucleus of a trading floor, I suggest you pay one a visit when you begin work on Wall Street. Tourists are not allowed to go into the heart of it, but as a developer for a company that has traders on the floor, you're given certain benefits. It's an experience to remember. Do the traders in the pit run around yelling all day like you see on TV? Well, no. In fact, much of the day is very, very quiet, with occasional bursts of insane lunacy. During the long stretches of calm, traders often play electronic card games (online poker is very, very popular).

The trading desk is an exhausting place to work. There is a lot of pacing going on. Traders tend to just stick a wireless phone appliance to their head and pace while talking to clients. Depending on your outlook, this is either mildly amusing or extremely unnerving. It's difficult to code anywhere near the area. There is constant yelling; something that requires more endurance and skill than you may realize, and something that a few traders practice before the trading day begins (absolute truth). There is little rest for the entire day. Some banks even have 'water runners' who bring water bottles to the trading stations so that the traders don't have to leave their posts. Now think about being a trader in this situation, loading your trading screen in the morning, and being presented with a completely different UI layout because some newbie hotshot programmer decided it looked cooler.

Large banks vs. small hedge funds

My first job on Wall Street was at a very, very small company. When I joined, the place was ran by 5 partners - experienced IT guys who worked as developers in the financial arena for years prior to this. This is rather rare, actually. Most small Wall Street companies are founded by ex-business guys and traders who did well for themselves years before. But this was a trading shop ran by programmers, and it made things a bit easier to deal with in retrospect.

Over the years, whenever asked about the single best piece of advice I can give to recent college graduates looking to get into Wall Street as developers, I never hesitate to answer: prefer small companies to large investment banks.

I cannot stress enough how important it is for entry-level developers to begin their careers in smaller Wall Street firms.

While the international investment banks will provide you with security (assuming you still believe there is such a thing), you will not be able to absorb nearly as much information as you would working for a smaller company. And the type of skills and information you gain working for a smaller company will translate directly to the amount of choice and leverage you'll have later on in your career.

The single most important factor to which I attribute my success on Wall Street (ahem...), is that I began my career working for a tiny market maker firm.

As an example, let's say a typical entry-level candidate with a solid understanding of Computer Science, a medium grasp of C++, and absolutely no knowledge of anything in the financial arena decides to jump into a career as a programmer on Wall Street.

After two years of working in a large, international investment bank with 20,000 other people, the candidate attains a pretty good understanding of financial products. He also gains a substantial amount of inter-office social skills (mostly as a result of office politics), a healthy respect for a slower-than-necessary development and release process, and the belief that it is an absolute requirement to have two weeks worth of meetings in order to approve a change to a single environment variable in a configuration file. His debugging skills probably improve, but his programming skills, after reaching a certain plateau of mediocrity, are no longer competitive. Ask him what he learned from the experience, and he will spew the same corporate advertisement that he was sold on originally - *a vibrant, diverse, exciting environment where you get the chance to work with some of the most brilliant people in the industry, and build a solid career for yourself in the process.*

Bull shit...

Even while this generic, corporate nonsense leaves his mouth he realizes that the only thing he remembers doing the whole time is sitting in meetings about meetings, and writing the same SQL stored procedure over and over.

After two years working at a small company, on the other hand, the candidate reaches a painfully thorough understanding of a small area of the financial world - whatever happens to be the focus of the company he worked for. He gains the same level of inter-office social skills (office politics cannot be avoided...anywhere). He also gains excellent debugging skills through analyzing raw Solaris core dumps on a daily basis, and gains environment foundation skills by constantly having to tweak Rendezvous channels, Sybase settings, Solaris process heap sizes, XML configuration files, and logging frameworks - all in a live production environment. He also learns 'trader speak' – something that will serve him greatly no matter where he goes, by having to deal with traders both in the work setting, and the occasional after-work social setting. He learns how to build, debug, deploy and maintain code, which he is entirely responsible for, from scratch. He learns how to diagnose a problem in production, make the fix in the code, and release it as a patch within minutes of it being reported to him (usually by a screaming trader from across the room). He also picks up about 4 new programming languages, including C (because most third-party trading libraries require it), some shell language (because there is always a need), Perl (because soon after learning a shell language, he decided it sucked), and a *really* good understanding of SQL (using **sqh**, or **isql** from the command line - because production servers do not have a cushy UI to work with).

I've come across developers whose skills, having joined a large investment bank straight out of school, simply don't compare to those of mid-level developers coming out of a small company with 3 or 4 years of experience. Starting out your career in a small company is akin to being thrown into the pool when learning how to swim. If you can't handle it, well, I'm sure you'll have no trouble getting into a large bank anyway. But if you succeed, your practical skills will be orders of magnitude higher than those of candidates coming out of investment banks.

Finally, there is one other aspect of big banks that most people don't concern themselves with before accepting an offer.

The Big Brother factor...

What does it take for a bank to stay in business for over 100 years? Luck? Brilliant management? Motivated employees?

Well yes, but many companies have that, and not all of them manage to stay put for over a century.

The answer is: *reputation*.

The big banks of Wall Street care about maintaining their reputation in good standing above all else. A bad trade can be covered in time, but an employee doing something that harms the bank's reputation brings consequences that will linger for years to come. Over the years, there have been several cases of greedy or disgruntled employees doing things that brought their firms to their knees in the eyes of Wall Street, and the media. And each year, firms that have not been damaged in such a way yet, or have managed, over a long time, to rebuild their reputations, get more and more paranoid about jeopardizing their reputations - especially through employee negligence.

But therein lays the dilemma. How do you run a firm with thirty thousand employees, and ensure that none of them embezzle money, or leak sensitive information to the media, or get involved in illegal deals with competitive companies, or break some compliance rule, or do any other dumb thing to put the reputation of the firm at risk?

Control is the answer. And attempts at controlling the behavior of thousands of people in a monitored environment, is what some people - as a reference to Orwell - would refer to as the Big Brother factor.

The implementation?

Personal brokerage and trading accounts are not allowed. All such accounts are to be closed shortly after joining the firm. If you wish to do any personal market trading while employed at the firm, you may do so only through the firm itself - usually with restrictions such as the minimum amount of time you are required to hold a position. In short - no day trading.

All personal published writing, creative, technical and otherwise is to be approved by the firm before being submitted to an editor for publication. It doesn't make a difference if the firm is mentioned in the piece or not. Whether it's a tutorial covering some new topic in technology, or a monthly column you write on the side for a gardening magazine, it has to meet with the firm's approval before being published. In fact, check with the legal department before starting to write it. In fact, forget about writing it altogether - you're an employee of The Bank now, you shouldn't have any outside endeavors.

As you can probably tell, I've had some issues with Big Brother in the past over some of my published writing, and I subsequently resigned my position because of it.

Digging around in other people's code should be praised, not scolded. If you have the curiosity, and the skills to go deep into the logic of the networking layer in order to find out what really happens to those packets you send through all of those fantastic abstractions, you should, by all means, be able to do so. Nevertheless, in large banks, if the immediate layers of management above your head are not themselves capable or inclined to learn about any technology outside their specific domains, they certainly don't want people 'below' them to know more than they do, and they will let you know immediately that lurking around in foreign code, for your own 'amusement' is strongly discouraged.

All web activity is monitored. All web content is filtered. Most of it is restricted. No blogs, no media content, and no entertainment sites. Browsing to any page not having anything to do with work – in fact, browsing to any page outside the company intranet – is strongly discouraged.

An internal facility is provided for submitting requests to open up a restricted site...but doing so, is strongly discouraged.

All instant messaging clients (web based and desktop) are disabled. Good luck even trying to install one. Good luck even trying to open up a web page containing a link to one. Making repeated attempts at finding an obscure way of installing or downloading such software is strongly discouraged.

Email accounts outside of work are not accessible. This includes any attempts to access an outside POP server, all public web-based email, as well as private or collegiate web-based email systems. Attempting to circumvent these restrictions is strongly discouraged.

All incoming and outgoing employee email is monitored. An 'unhealthy' amount of email not dealing with work related matters is scrutinized and strongly discouraged.

Email signatures of the most mundane and benign kind are considered too risqué, and are, of course, strongly discouraged.

The enforcement?

An entire floor of people whose sole job is to monitor and restrict network traffic, as well as a legal and compliance department whose job is to make sure you know what 'strongly discouraged' really means.

Small firms have none of this. They're too busy trying to make something of themselves to worry about some employee occasionally reading a Dilbert comic online or posting a blog entry depicting the latest adventures of his cat.

The consequences?

College kids who join big banks out of school tend to stay there for a long time. It's cushy, the bonuses grow with each year, and the work is, frankly, not that hard. Experienced developers tend to flee after a few months. Some are appalled by the level of bureaucracy. Some can't stand being constantly 'monitored'. Some are irritated at the fact that they have to have every single line of code pass through a gauntlet of red tape before it sees a production machine. Most are simply bored out of their skulls and leave to pursue something more intellectually stimulating.

Many large companies lose experienced developers even before they have a chance to make them an offer. This is bureaucracy at work again. It's not uncommon for the initial interview to include only a few people from the group, with as many as 6 or 7 additional required interviews taking place over the course of a month before a decision is made and the candidate is given an offer. This type of nonsense may work for an entry-level developer looking for his first job, but experienced developers are too heavily bombarded with other offers to wait a month for one bank. Eventually, the experienced candidate will simply decide to take another offer rather than wait for the big bank to get its wheels rolling with a hiring decision.

When I interviewed at one such bank, I made it clear to my recruiter and to the department I was interviewing with that I already had another offer in store, and that if they weren't capable of making their decision after a single interview, I wouldn't be interested in joining. Even though they put me through a 9-hour interview gauntlet that day, they were able to make a decision after only a single interview session – and I received an offer the next morning.

You don't have to settle for what others are accustomed to. There is no *right* way to do things here. You are *not* a generic peg in the production line of Wall Street (even though the work may make you feel that way at times), and there's no reason why you should hesitate to set your own terms in any negotiation.

I have a theory that the average level of intelligence in large investment banks is lower as compared with smaller firms, precisely because of their failure to recruit and retain hardcore, experienced developers. But alas, it is only a theory.

All this talk about the benefits of smaller companies doesn't mean that smaller companies are *always* the way to go.

There is certainly more stability of a certain kind to be found in larger investment banks. All else being equal - meaning your performance is adequate as an employee of a firm of any size - the chances of a small company going belly up are higher, compared to that of a large investment bank that has been in business for over 100 years. Anything could happen, and even this is not a sure thing, but you don't see many international banks close shop all too often, whereas I've had three of the smaller firms I worked in close their doors soon after I came aboard (let's just assume that this wasn't an indication of anything on my part).

There is less opportunity for training in smaller firms. Big banks provide facilities for building knowledge in domains where you think you need improvement. If you want to catch up on your business skills, or knowledge of a certain financial instrument, or simply improve personal productivity, the larger banks host classes and seminars that you can attend. Smaller firms have none of this. If you want to learn, open a book, or take a night class at a local college.

Some small companies are founded entirely by business types, and IT is treated as somewhat of an afterthought. If you find yourself in one of these places – especially if you're one of the first programmers in the place – be warned, they are probably only now realizing that their growth has been severely limited by their inability to leverage technology. The situation you are getting yourself into is one where they want the world from you, as a developer, but at the same time, they don't really know what they want.

Up until you came aboard, their pinnacle of technology was the occasional Excel macro one of them managed to record by keystroke. This doesn't stop them from thinking that they know everything there is to know about programming, the IT world in general, and about the kind of work you do as a programmer specifically. This is where being a young, inexperienced developer can get you in trouble. Even some experienced developers (myself included) have had problems working in places like this.

The clues begin to trickle in during the initial interviews. *"What we've been doing so far, is writing our orders down on pieces of paper, you see, and handing them off to our operations officer...and this has worked great for us"*. At this point, you look across the hall at this operations officer and see a look of pure exhaustion on his face - that, and 27 empty coffee cups on his desk.

"But we are trying to expand, we don't think that he will be able to carry the work load, so what we really need, is a fully automated trading system." Alright - you think to yourself - this will be great! I get to hack together an entire trading system from scratch with my own design, and when they expand and bring more programmers onboard, I will be master of the domain, since I will have built the entire thing by myself and I'll know it inside and out. This will look great on my résumé!

Well...we'll see. Let's go on with the interview…

After the four or five partners of the firm interview you, you begin to realize that while they all agree that they need "a trading system", you've been given seven different general specs from five different people. One of them wants something simple to handle a few trades, but wants it to be done yesterday, since they "really need it". Another one wants a solid, generic, fully extendible system that will support unlimited upgrades in case they want greater functionality later on – and he doesn't care how long it takes to build, as long as it's solid. This third wants something different entirely.

But you don't let this stop you. I'll build the best system out there, you think to yourself. After all, I'll have no-one around to critique my work or tell me how to do things. I'll do it my way, and it'll be the best piece of software on Wall Street.

"*Can you do this?*" they ask.

"*SURE!*" you exclaim...and you accept the position.

That night, you have some doubts, but you convince yourself that it's just new-job-jitters. You say to yourself, "S*elf, there is nothing to be afraid of. You are trained for this, and you have a few years of experience under your belt. You've worked on teams before where you helped build trading systems. You can do anything you want with the* *design. You can even pick the language to write it in. Wow - you can write the thing in Lisp, and no-one will object. Everything will be cool."*

And everything is cool...for a while.

When you begin your new job, you realize what "no IT department" really means. There are no servers, no networking, no CVS tree, and no software licenses - for anything. So you spend you first few weeks ordering, configuring and integrating some servers, setting up firewalls, ordering some essential software, and setting up the source code repository. It's not exactly in the job description...but you don't mind. Not yet, anyway.

The following week, one of the partners sits down with you and tells you that they have a better idea of what they want. He had spent the past weekend browsing for off-the-shelf trading systems on the internet and found a few that he likes. He loads up a browser and shows you a few of them. *"We want this feature, and that one. It also has to be able to do this, import from here, export to that, send confirmations, and keep all history for compliance purposes. How long will it take you to do this?"*

Umm....

And here's the pivotal point.

"*A YEAR! It'll take a friggin' year at least!*" yells the pragmatic programmer inside your head. Of course, you don't listen to that fool. What does he know? He didn't just land a spectacular job like this. He only knows silly things based on previous experience. Things about proper software development, proper unit testing, proper code documentation, and proper code reviews. Somewhere in there, he also knows a thing or two about estimating project timelines, but you don't listen to him.

How can you tell your new boss that this thing will take a year to write? He'll laugh at you before throwing you out of the building. These guys think that programming only requires a few keyboard clicks – same as recording those Excel macros - and the only reason they hired a programmer is because they consider the task much too intellectually inferior to what they do, to even consider learning anything about it. You can't tell them it'll take a year!

So you tell them you can have a bare-bones version of something useful within 2 months or so. It won't do much, but it will swallow up the basic trade types, do some simple validation and store the data in a database.

"But this off-the-shelf system I just showed you from this other company has all these other features. Can you do this as well?"

And you think to yourself: *"This off-the-shelf system he just showed me had 30 programmers working on it for over 2 years, and it sells for $850,000 per license. He must be insane."*

But he's not insane. He just lacks the fundamental understanding of what a single programmer is capable of. He has no way of knowing any of it. He has never worked with developers, and the company has never had an IT department before. If, at this point, you don't begin to realize that it is just as much your job to educate these people about what is possible and what isn't, as it is to actually build what they are asking of you, your life there will be more miserable than it would have been, have you joined a large investment bank.

So you start on the project, and you realize just how much needs to be done before a single line of actual trading system code is written. A database has to be designed and implemented. A logging layer of some sort has to be written. A messaging layer of sorts has to be designed and implemented, because while they may not realize it yet, if one trader submits a trade through his trading screen, all the other traders should be able to see this trade in their screens. Now you have a distributed system. And this requires a messaging layer – unless you want to write low level TCP or UDP socket code every time you need to send or receive a packet of data.

So now you need a messaging layer, a logging facility, a database interface layer, a rudimentary release system, and the skeleton code for at least one server and one client. And all of this will take much more time than you think. Do you really think it's trivial to write a stable messaging system? You are about to enter multithreaded, distributed, mutex hell for the next two months - at the end of which, you won't even have one single widget to display on the screen for the traders, because all of this stuff is foundation work.

But at the end of two months they won't care about the foundation work. The trading system in their minds has a screen with buttons they can press to do something.

And this is where you begin to lose them. You know you're doing good work. In fact, you may have just surpassed all programming speed records known to man to build this foundation layer. But they don't care. In time, they may begin to realize that they had unrealistic expectations, and that you, in fact, may be working very hard indeed. But it's too late. You failed to meet the original expectations - no matter how absurd they were. They didn't know at the time that a trading system them wanted would take more than a year to build. And you didn't tell them. Even if they know this now, you're no longer the golden boy they hired.

Maybe you should have taken that cushy cubicle gig at the large investment bank across the street? After all, they've had an IT department for years, and their expectations are no-where as high.

The programming environment

The foundation of a typical development environment consists of a single UNIX box, or a shared cluster of UNIX machines - as well as one dedicated Windows machine per developer. The UNIX box, in all likelihood, will be a Solaris workstation - one that is at least one generation behind. If you are working in a younger company (or a more technologically aware one), you'll have access to a Linux machine as well.

The main purpose of the Windows machine is Outlook. Don't let anyone tell you that Microsoft Word is the reason the population sticks with Windows. Nonsense. It's the masses using Exchange Server with Outlook.

Years ago, I made an attempt to get rid of my Windows machine at work by switching from Outlook to Pine. This failed. Actually, what I really wanted to do was to stay exclusively in UNIX so that I could play NetHack in the background without anyone noticing. This failed as well.

On UNIX systems, your compiler will be the ubiquitous **gcc**. In older shops, you may have a few users of the Sun Workshop suite as well, the Java enthusiasts will work with whatever they have, and the few Windows shops will, of course, rely on Visual Studio.

The debugger will be **gdb** or **dbx** on UNIX, and, once again, the excellent Visual Studio debugger on Windows - about the only thing I actually like about that IDE.

Source code control will be **cvs**, or **sccs**. No one here apparently trusts **subversion** yet, and no one *really* uses SourceSafe. If you are using SourceSafe, and you still have a smidge of hacker spirit in you, you're either using it under threat of physical torture, or Bill promised to reward you with a harem at some point.

The layout tool is still Visio - or in my case - an archaic device known as a pencil, which works amazingly well with an analog medium known as a piece of paper.

The monitors are tragic at best. For as long as I can remember, I've had better monitors at home than at any firm I've worked in.

The networking layer is Tibco, with a bit of Rendezvoud on top of UDP. This is almost ubiquitous, so I won't even mention the few shops using other alternatives.

The C++ library is either STL, RogueWave, or, more likely, a messy proprietary set of classes which just barely work together - only because everything is implemented in header files and you can always change the hash table logic to suit your needs.

At one point, developers were taught enough in academia to be able to write hash tables from scratch (as well as memory managers). This seems to be no longer the case. Why should the size of a hash table preferably be a prime number? Look it up.

The system you'll be working on will be distributed - in theory, but in practice, the whole thing will feel like a monolithic application. Let me explain. There is no single application per-se. All components of the system are UDP packet pushers; communicating through the network. There may be as few as 5 components, or as many as 100 - each doing separate tasks within the flow of a single trade. One component is responsible for sending quotes to the market. Another component is responsible for receiving prices. Another one deals with risk management. Another receives trade confirmations. Something resolves trader permissions, something deals with clearing, and something else deals with back-office allocations.

The problem is that none of these separate components can work without the others. In a well-designed distributed system, this would be the case, but this is Wall Street, and things just need to compile, run, and make money for the firm.

Managing the development environment itself on a daily basis can be a pretty frustrating exercise in futility. There are days when you get nothing done because you're trying to get all the components to work together properly - but your deadlines still persist. As a programmer, you should be responsible for your code, not for system maintenance and stability, but sometimes it's easier to just fix it yourself than to hunt down the person responsible. Many developers leave firms because of atrocious development environments.

So if you're facing a system like this, where do you, as a developer, stand on a daily basis when you get into work in the morning? Well. Let me take you through a typical day of surviving a Wall Street programming environment.

My task on this day, for the sake of argument, is to test a simple option trade on the ISE (International Securities Exchange).

- I come into the office.

- Did everything compile from last night? Of course not. OK. Recompile - 30 minutes.

- That piece of code that connects to the ISE core dumps upon launch. Why? Oh yeah, someone upgraded something in the messaging layer, and none of the data types align properly anymore. 2 hours to figure this out, after which I grab the old version of the messaging layer and compile the connection code against that.

- The code connects...but the ISE test environment is down. Call ISE support - they're in the middle of an upgrade - wait 20 minutes.

- The code connects...but there are no prices in the ISE test environment to work against. Market rules state that you can't trade against yourself, so I need fake prices. I either have to call the ISE again, this time to get them to populate the fake market with fake prices, or I need a way to simulate fake prices myself. Of course, no-one had enough foresight to implement a simple mechanism where I can record incoming data to a text file, and simply replay the flow when I have no real data to work with. There go 2 more hours.

- The UI through which I can send a test trade is not working properly. I dig up an old command-line script to send a fake trade. After 15 minutes of trying to figure out the usage of the script, I open the code itself and realize that the usage printout hasn't been updated since the last 20 revisions of the code. So I spend another 10 minutes trying to decipher what it is that the script actually wants for parameters.

- Alright! The fake trade went through. It seemed to have passed through the first few layers without a hitch, but fails to book. What could be the problem now?!

- Ahh! The module checking for product consistency is not running. I start that process and hope it works, since I've never worked on this piece of code, and the guy that did called in sick. It seems to have started...let's try to send the trade again.

- The trade fails. The logs seem to indicate some sort of a duplication error. I've seen this before!

- I flush the pipeline to get rid of the old pending trade and send it again.

- The trade fails. Three out of the six required processes in the trade path were built overnight against the new messaging library - my code was not, and of course, no-one else is around. I check out all three modules and build them from scratch to match the version of the messaging layer against which my own code was built. At this point, it's about 5 hours into the work day - and I haven't accomplished anything.

- The code finished building and linking. I launch the processes and send the trade through.

- The trade looks like it went through properly, but I can't find it anywhere in the system. It's not showing up anywhere down the pipe. After a quick check of the log files, I fail to find a problem. No errors...damn. What do I do now?

- I increase the debug logging levels to get more detailed output and bounced all the processes before resending the trade.

- It failed because the Rendezvous channels are all screwed up. Some other poor developer on another floor has been receiving weird option trades all this time. He can't get any work done because he gets strange trades that are not his own, and I can't get any work done because my data is going to his machine. I resolve the Rendezvous channels and send the trade through again.

- OK. It sort of worked. The trade is in the database, but all the values are incorrect. Why does this new option expire in 1973? That can't be right. How is this possible? Network issue? Calendar library issue? Something in my own code? Where, in this mess of code contained in six different modules (that I know about) is this bug?

- But I'm much too tired to deal with this today. It's already been 10 hours. I'm just happy that the trade went through...who cares about the actual data.

A week later the code goes into production and all the incoming data is wrong. Why? After 30 minutes of having traders yell at you over the phone, you realize that the fake ISE market behaves nothing like the real ISE market - the real market has slightly different products, slightly different dynamics, and 100 times more data to deal with. The production code gets rolled back - and it's entirely your fault - of course.

Welcome to Wall Street.

Typical day - then and now

When I was still in school, the one question I always wanted to get an answer to was - what is it that programmers do all day long? I wasn't looking for a generic - "a programmer is responsible for..." type of answer, I really wanted to know the full breakdown of what a typical day as a programmer was like.

I still ask myself this question when it comes to professions I am not a part of. What do police officers and firefighters do all day long? What about investigative reporters? And repo men! It would probably be a blast to sit down with a repo man and dig into some of his stories. But I digress.

So what is it that Wall Street programmers do all day?

Giving it a bit of thought, I'm tempted to say...nothing. But, alas, this would be equivalent of a child's answer when a parent inquires as to what he did in school the whole day. And since you'd probably prefer to actually have a practical answer rather than to be satisfied with a copout response like that, I'd better give it more than just a bit of thought.

The easiest way for me to answer this question is to compare a day I remember when I first started my career to a day that occurred recently, after some years have passed. The following two days really occurred. I consider these to be good examples of typical days on the job. Nothing has been fabricated, and if memory serves correctly, nothing has been omitted either.

Typical day at my first job

To put things in some context, this was a very small market maker firm on Wall Street. They traded options on futures, and I was responsible for building the various communication layers between the company's systems and the outside exchanges. It was managed by five IT guys and a few traders. Aside from the IT partners, there were about four additional programmers - and I was the newest. I had proposed to my girlfriend just a few short weeks prior to this, and am, understandably, floating on cloud nine. There's nothing like getting that first job and realizing that you can now actually afford to get married.

7:30 AM - Wake up. Shower. Get dressed; which at this point means putting on worn jeans and a shirt that smells least like it was sitting in a pile on the floor amongst other shirts. Grab some coffee, and run to the bus.

8:30 AM - Arrive on Wall Street. I didn't know at this point that the one hour commute I endure every day would turn out to be the shortest of all the commutes to come. Exit the bus. Buy another cup of coffee. Have a cigarette (yes, I know, I know. I actually quit for seven years at one point...but started again after I joined one of those large investment banks). Go inside the office building.

8:35 AM - Say hello and throw a nod to the CTO, who is sitting in a corner, coding with his headphones on. He ignores me completely. I sit down, log into my Solaris account, and put on my own headphones.

8:40 AM - Check email quickly - nothing - good. Fire up vi (not vim, or *gasp* Emacs), and started implementing some brilliant bug fix I thought of in the shower that morning.

9:15 AM - Some trader is freaking out because his computer is not working properly. It's now fifteen minutes before the opening bell rings. I go see what the problem is...

9:16 AM - The trader left the caps-lock activated on his Sun keyboard. Solaris doesn't play well with the caps-lock key, so things began acting strangely. This actually happens every week - three times at least with this trader alone. I turn the caps-lock key off, and go back to my workstation.

9:17 AM - My cubicle neighbor comes in. I tell him about the trader, and we laugh for a solid 10 minutes.

9:30 AM - Trading starts. The trading room is now about as quiet as an airplane hangar. I put on my headphones and continue to hack code.

11:00 AM - I go out for a cigarette and another cup of coffee. It's only about three months after I completed my degree and ended the nightmarish week of finals during which time I've been living on about 10 gallons of coffee a day. The local 7-11 kept a pot warm for me the whole night, knowing that I would be dropping by for a refill at around 3 AM. Three months have now passed, but I still can't kick the coffee habit entirely. I come back to the office, put on my headphones and resumé coding.

12:00 PM - I run to the gym for 20 minutes, after which I have lunch with a friend, grab another cigarette (completely disregarding the 20 minute treadmill session), as well as another cup of coffee, before coming back to the office. I check my email - there is a mandatory API upgrade due in 3 months - fine. Log this into a .txt file, put on my headphones and start coding again.

1:00 PM - Cigarette and coffee.

2:00 PM - Cigarette and coffee.

2:20 PM - The development environment went haywire, so I can't code. It's time for a cigarette and some more coffee.

3:45 PM - The dev environment is now up...barely; back to coding.

4:30 PM - The CTO sends out an email informing me that since the traders are particularly annoyed today (something about the keyboard not working this morning), they want that new feature I've been working on by end of trading day tomorrow. Crap! I guess I'm staying late tonight...again.

6:00 PM - It finally compiles!

7:15 PM - Now it compiles and doesn't core dump!

7:20 PM - Quick run ... good. Quick test ... good. Commit the code, and submit a release request ticket.

7:22 PM - Run to catch the last bus.

7:24 PM - Missed the last bus...

7:30 PM - Take the subway home...

9:00 PM - Get home. Have a cigarette. Grab a quick PB&J sandwich. Watch some TV.

11:30 PM - Sleep.

2:00 AM - Have a dream where I am Pac Man, and the traders are the little ghosts chasing me.

Typical day at a recent job

It's now a few years and 1,000,000 coffee cups later. On this day, I am working at a large, international, investment bank - several months into the job.

5:00 AM - Alarm goes off. I hit the snooze button.

5:10 AM - I hit the snooze button again.

5:20 AM - My wife hits me since I wake her up every ten minutes. I get up, accidentally stepping on the cat in the process, and tell myself to try to get to bed earlier from now on as the screaming cat proceeds to scratch me in retaliation. I turn the alarm off...I've grown to despise that sound.

5:30 AM - Shower.

5:45 AM - I get dressed. Pants, shirt, tie, jacket. I distinctly remember owning a pair of jeans.

6:10 AM - Walk the dog. Pick up dog poop. Have a cigarette (a habit I recently returned to). Have a cup of coffee, and catch five minutes of the morning news. Those guys have no right being that happy this early in the morning.

6:30 AM - Leave the house. Check the blackberry - 37 new messages.

6:45 AM - Grab the subway and attempt to answer 37 email messages from the road.

7:30 AM - Exit the subway. Grab some breakfast and a cigarette.

8:00 AM - Arrive at the office. Sit in a two hour meeting about absolutely nothing.

10:00 AM - Check email - 26 new messages. The development environment is down again...not that it really matters at this point.

10:05 AM - Cigarette and coffee.

10:30 AM - Another meeting - also about nothing.

12:00 PM - Lunch. It's never as healthy as it should be. I call my wife. Then I call the cat and the dog. Yes, I do that. You can call me weird, but I already know that. Besides, I love my animals...they're family. Have a cigarette. A quick run to the gym? Nah...

1:20 PM - Meetings happen. This is a meeting to cover the points made at the 8 AM meeting. Yes, these actually occur. This is a perfect opportunity to point out that you never really need to be awake for the 8 AM meeting since there's always an encore around the corner.

1:55 PM - The development environment is back up. I fix one line of code in a stored procedure, and then proceed to yell at the DBA for turning off the login I always use to access the database. I don't care about protocol, security and standards! I *like* logging in as the database owner!

2:10 PM - Get my database access restored by the DBA. Hah! Check the new stored procedure, commit the code and submit it to QA. One line of code change...sheesh. I used to program for a living!

2:30 PM - Interview a new candidate for an entry-level position.

3:00 PM - Interview an intern for an open summer spot.

3:30 PM - The proprietary infrastructure UDP messaging layer is broken. What else is new? I wish I could meet the original writer of this thing. I read network packet debug logs for the next 2 hours.

5:50 PM - I fix a 1-off error in some socket code, compile the thing, and submit an emergency release ticket. No one can do any work while the patch is being applied.

6:00 PM - Cigarette and coffee with an old friend. This is really why I still come to work.

6:15 PM - Meeting about the release strategy for tonight.

7:00 PM - Small mid-week release started.

7:20 PM - The release was reasonably uneventful.

7:23 PM - Spoke too soon. Three processes can't access the database. The DBA screwed something up when he was mucking around with permissions earlier in the day.

9:00 PM - Everything is finally stable after a 90 minute phone-tag session with the release squad and the DBA.

9:15 PM - Check email - 63 new messages. Ignore them all.

9:20 PM - Catch the company car outside - get driven home.

9:40 PM - Get home. Have dinner with my wife. Walk the dog. Apologize to the cat. Watch some crap on TV.

10:30 PM - Sleep.

2:00 AM - Have a dream where I am Pac Man, and everyone in the office is a little blue ghost that I can chase and eat.

Random advice
(or, things I wish I knew before I signed up for this)

Your tools will suck ... get over it

On Wall Street, programmers are often seen as a necessary expense, so unless the shop is ran by a group of developers, which is rarely the case, your tools at home, including your monitors, your workstations, and probably your chairs, will be better than the ones you're provided with at the office. If you work at a smaller firm, these things will be a bit better than in large investment banks. This is partly because firms just starting out tend to want to look big, and buying expensive equipment makes them look it - at least in their own eyes, and partly because in larger investment banks, equipment is often rotated from department to department, and replaced only on rare need, with request forms having to be filled out in triplicate, and other such nonsense. Software is an altogether different animal. If you put your case forward with enough force, you can usually get the programmer's editor of your choice (especially if the firm already has a few licenses floating around), but you'll probably be spending most of your time in UNIX with vi (vim), Emacs, gdb, and eclipse (if you're hacking java code).

For recent college grads - no one here is your mommy

You will get that feeling. I know you will. You'll arrive all excited and hopeful, see the level of intensity of an actual workplace, and find yourself wishing for a mentor of some sort; a person who can provide you with some cover, some patient explanations, and a general friendship for your first few months of dread.

This is a very natural feeling; your decisions here do not result in a class grade; they result in some trader being able to depend on your code to make enough living to feed his family.

You might reach tears when lying in bed that first night after you come home from work...I have. Maybe this is because you did have a foul experience on your first day, but it's mostly the realization of the amount of responsibility that you now have on your shoulders. This is a new feeling, and unless you had some hard times in your life prior to leaving college, this new type of responsibility is something you'll have to get used to.

Welcome to adulthood.

Finding a mentor is very difficult to achieve. These people are not here to help you...not in the way you want them to. Your best bet is a 'sibling' of sort. Find someone close to your age group and attach yourself to him for a few months. You might wind up working with him time and time again as your career matures. Wall Street is a very small place.

Most projects will suck

There are very few truly interesting projects here. Most of the work is client-server code, and most of that is cleaning up outdated spaghetti code. This is just how it is, and I'm sure it's not limited to Wall Street. You are working in an enterprise environment where the product line is internal, interconnected, revolving, and long-standing. And unlike shrink-wrapped application development, the finished product is not the end, but only a means to an end - the happy trader and a profitable quarter. If you seek the feeling of writing something from scratch, with an original, clean design, then join or start an open-source project on the side (assuming you find the time), or you can just wait a bit – original and unique projects do come around on Wall Street once in a while.

Go out for drinks

You'll start on a Monday morning, and by the Friday of the same week one of your colleague will have asked you to join the rest of the team for drinks after work. Please understand. If you care about your tenure at the firm, you have absolutely, positively, no choice in the matter; you have to go.

If you don't go, because you don't want to, or because you genuinely have other plans, you risk alienating yourself and making your future life at that firm more miserable than it has to be. After-work drinks are as much a part of Wall Street life as the opening bell.

If you're going out with some traders, they'll most likely be drinking Guinness. Now, I can't stand the stuff; it's too bitter for my taste and heavy enough to be a full meal. You can try the Guinness, you can order a glass of Brandy (like I do), or you can refrain from drinking altogether, but you really should join them if asked - at least the first few times.

Buy a good pair of headphones

Oh boy....just trust me on this. Coding in an office anywhere within a few miles of a trading floor is not the same as coding at home...it's not even the same as coding at a Nirvana concert (did I date myself too much with that reference?) Buy a good pair of headphones for yourself and allocate a bit of cash in your budget for some music.

Interview with a Wall Street programmer

Lenny Primak is one of the smartest developers working on Wall Street today. I had the good fortune to work with him at one point, and he continues to be a friend and mentor through the years. I asked him if he would do a quick interview for this book, and he agreed.

Lenny was something of a child prodigy - or so he claims. His first paying programming job was at the age of sixteen, and his first programming gig on Wall Street arrived two years later. He became a consultant for financial firms at the age of twenty-two, and never looked back.

Lenny also holds a number of patents for technologies I'll never be smart enough to understand, and carries a pilot's license (although he'd never drag me into a plane with him).

Was it your intent to work on Wall Street as a developer, or did it come about as a result of unexpected circumstances?

It was my intent to be a programmer, doing interesting things. When I was an up-and-coming programmer, the 'Holy Grail' for NY programming (or what seemed like the Holy Grail at the time) was being a programmer on Wall Street. I love programming, and it doesn't really matter whether it's for trading, trucking or singing. It's awesome!

Do you prefer working for a small company or a large bank?

Small company. A lot of large companies stifle innovation and have a lot of baggage in place - although, I've been able to circumvent this as of late, by creating a microcosm in my own group where I am really operating creatively with my own rules. This is done largely by making arrangements to work from home most of the time. This isn't really feasible for most people, but do try! I do love working for small companies. They are usually nimble, innovative and market-driven.

It's easy to innovate and be creative.

How would you rate the level of satisfaction that you get from your career?

Career? I have no career. There is no such thing as a career anymore. If a company keeps you around 'just because', it's a stupid company and you don't want to work there anyway. They should keep you as long as it makes sense. If not they should lay you off. I expect to be fired (laid off if you are a permanent employee) every day I come to work. Stay as long as it makes sense. Leave if it doesn't. Even if you have kids to feed, you will land on your feet; there is a high enough demand for skilled people. Don't live for work. Work to live!

What is the most challenging project that you ever worked on?

I once had a project to figure out dividends for a price-weighted index. I actually had to write down a data description tree that was 10 levels deep. I could not have figured it out without a piece of paper. Never again (and never before) have I resorted to such tactics – a full page data tree. That was intense. I had templates 4 levels deep and another 3 levels of indirection, with lots of ***asserts***. This was during my C++ days, but I would have done the same thing with Java generics today.

What do you consider to be the worst part of the job?

Getting up in the morning. Just don't do it! Also, having to explain the same thing to people ten times.

What do you consider to be the most boring part of the job?

Boring? I am never bored. When I don't have enough to do, I do stuff for myself.

What do you consider to be the most exciting part of the job?

It's definitely the challenge. It's challenging to be creative. It's challenging to solve different problems in the simplest way possible. Fitting into a 24 hour day is a challenge. Conveying your thoughts to people and fitting the knowledge into their brains is a challenge. Writing good code is a challenge. I love a challenge - bring it on!

Describe some of the responsibilities/roles you've had over the years.

I've never cleaned toilets. But I am not above it - as long as they pay me! From DBA, to SA, to data cleaner, to manager of 80 people, to code refactorer.

Do you enjoy dealing with traders or other 'customers' of Wall Street?

Just say no to them! They always want everything right now. Just say what's possible and don't give in. Underpromise and overdeliver.

If you could have any job in the world for any amount of money, would you choose to remain a Wall Street Programmer?

Playboy photographer and model scout. I'd even take a small pay cut. Astronaut. Wall Street Programmer. In that order.

Would your recommend to take the path of an employee or the path of an independent consultant?

It depends (probably on whether you have children). Health insurance is a big reason to be a permanent employee. Matching 401k is another. If none of this is an issue, or if you can swing it, being an independent consultant is the way to go. You can manage your own finances, and if you're good, you can save a significant chunk of money as compared to being an employee. I would only consider being an employee if a significant amount of stock/options would be on the table.

Any juicy tidbits or a great Wall Street software disaster story?

About 80% of projects I participated in were disasters. This isn't just me; most projects do fail. This isn't only true for Wall Street, it is true everywhere. To better frame this, I consider a project a success only when it has worked for more than 2 years and actually made money for the company. It's a high standard, but that's what it really takes.

So, what now?

You've now read everything I know about being a software developer on Wall Street. I learn new things on a daily basis, and will hopefully continue to do so as long as I keep hacking code here. Whether you are about to graduate from college and are looking to enter Wall Street as a programmer, or if you're an experienced developer thinking about transferring domains, I urge you to consider the things you've read here first, and perhaps speak with some of the friends you might have who work in the field. The last thing you want is to follow the glittering hype, only to find out that perhaps this isn't the place you thought it would be.

If you do decide to come work as a developer on Wall Street, look me up. I'd love to hear about your experiences. The beer is on me.

Cheers!